Another Day

365 Inspirational Poems

Billy Kyser, D.D.S.

ANOTHER DAY
Published by New Morning Publishing

Copyright © 2016 by Dr. Billy Kyser

All rights reserved.
Published in the United States of America.

No part of this book may be used or reproduced in any manner whatsoever without written permission except in the case of brief quotations embodied in critical articles and reviews.

Front cover Photo: ML Baxley Photography,
Used with permission.

Back cover photo: family photo. Used with permission.

Scripture quotations taken from the King James Bible, copyright © Cambridge University Press and Oxford University Press 1989. All rights reserved.

Scripture quotations taken from the New King James Bible, copyright © Cambridge University Press and Oxford University Press 1989. All rights reserved.

Scripture quotations taken from the New American Standard Bible, copyright © Cambridge University Press and Oxford University Press 1989. All rights reserved.

Scripture quotations marked (NIV) are taken from the Holy Bible, New International Version®, NIV®. Copyright © 2011 by Biblica, Inc.™ Used by permission of Zondervan. All rights reserved worldwide. www.zondervan.com The "NIV" and "New International Version" are trademarks registered in the United States Patent and Trademark Office by Biblica, Inc.™

Kyser, Billy.
Another Day
By Billy Kyser, D.D.S.

Dedications

To my wife, Peggy, the love of my life, for whom I wrote my first poem. You've inspired me for 56 years and have shown me how to truly serve the Lord.

To our daughter, Kim, and her husband, Ken, our sons, Scott and Chris, and our grandchildren, Brooks, Julia and Mason. To our future great-grandchildren and their children. I thank God for the blessing and legacy of each of you. We pray that all of you will know and love the Lord.

To my Heavenly Father, who bestowed upon me the gift of salvation and by His Holy Spirit inspired these verses.

Acknowledgements

I want to acknowledge my special friend Kathy Hedges who is at home in heaven celebrating with the Lord. Although she did not get to see the final printing, she encouraged me to begin the process and read many of the poems.

A very special thanks to Leslie Wilson for her editing expertise and for guiding me through the publication process.

To our daughter, Kim, for her hours of work and attention to details, thank you.

Two thumbs up to Randy Wolff who directed me to Leslie. He's a good friend and gifted, spiritual encourager.

And to Peggy, my wonderful wife and best friend for 56 years, thanks for being a sounding board for all that I have written.

Another Day

Billy Kyser

Rising early in the morning
with the world still quiet at rest
I watch the bright sun rising
and pray to do my best
God meets me there with open arms
and calms my troubled fears
like bursts of dawn He fills my soul
and brushes away my tears
He lifts me up through troubled waters
and guides me along the way
and I feel His presence there for me
throughout another day

January 1

The Greatest Love

For God so loved the world that he gave his only begotten son that whosoever believeth in him should not perish, but have everlasting life.
John 3:16 (KJV)

The greatest love the world has known
A sacrifice for what we've done
Was given by God to die on Calvary
A Lamb in the form of His Son

~~~

January 2

Fully Surrendered

But we all, with unveiled face, beholding as is a mirror the glory of the Lord, are being transformed into the same image from glory to glory, just as by the Spirit of the Lord.
2 Corinthians 3:18 (NKJV)

Lord, I surrender myself totally to thee
A bond servant forever, forgiven and free
Mold me and make me into what you want me to be
A reflection of Christ's love for others to see

January 3

Death's Gain

*For the wages of sin is death,
but the gift of God is eternal life
through Jesus Christ our Lord.*
Romans 6:23 (NIV)

A mourning heart brings floods of tears
But Jesus shares our pain
And gently reminds us, through the Holy Spirit,
That death is not loss but gain

January 4

The Lord's Refuge

*The blessing of the Lord, it maketh rich,
and he addeth no sorrow with it.*
Proverbs 10:22 (KJV)

Blessed are my ways in the refuge of the Lord
He comforts me when I pray
He carries my burdens and gently guides me
Through each and every day

January 5

God's Gifts to Me

Having then gifts differing according
to the grace that is given to us.
Romans 12:6a (KJV)

The gifts that God created for me
To be used wherever I can
Are tools for spreading the gospel of Christ
As part of His master plan

~~~

January 6

Treasures in Heaven

A man with an evil eye hastens after wealth,
and does not know that want will come upon him.
Proverbs 28:22 (NASB)

May all my work be for the Lord
Regardless of its worth
Storing all my treasures above in heaven
Instead of here on earth

January 7

My Shattered Life

*Blessed is he whose transgression is forgiven,
whose sin is covered.*
Psalm 32:1 (NKJV)

At the foot of the cross where Jesus died
I laid my shattered life
He restored it to order piece by piece
And covered my sin and strife

~~~

January 8

Help Those in Need

*They helped every one his neighbor;
and every one said to his brother,
be of good courage.*
Isaiah 41:6 (KJV)

Who have you helped in need today
Our Heavenly Father asks
The widows and poor each need a hand
His word gives us that task

January 9

His Only Son

For God so loved the world that he gave his only begotten son that whosoever believeth in him should not perish but have everlasting life.
John 3:16 (KJV)

God sent His only Son
To die on Calvary's tree
To suffer the penalty and offer salvation
To sinners like you and me

~~~

January 10

Wait for the Lord

But they that wait upon the Lord shall renew their strength; they shall mount up with wings like eagles; they shall run, and not be weary; and they shall walk, and not faint.
Isaiah 40:31 (KJV)

Wait for the Lord and walk in His ways
In all you say and do
And during the darkest storms of life
He'll safely guide you through

January 11

Delivered

The Lord is my light and my salvation;
whom shall I fear?
The Lord is the strength of my life;
of whom shall I be afraid?
Psalm 27:1 (KJV)

Once I was bound by the chains of sin
I wandered in darkness without sight
Then Jesus came and delivered me
And opened my eyes to the light

~~~

January 12

Our Savior's Comfort

Blessed are they that mourn;
for they shall be comforted.
Matthew 5:4 (KJV)

When the burdens of life bind our soul
And each day seems hopeless and vain
Turn for comfort to our risen Savior
He'll guide you through the pain

January 13

A Spirit of Giving

*For the poor shall never cease out of the land;
therefore I command thee saying,
Thou shalt open thine hand wide unto thy brother,
to thy poor, and to thy needy, in thy land.*
Deuteronomy 15:11 (KJV)

Lord give me the spirit of giving to others
That your light might shine through me
And reveal your love for the lost and needy
For all the world to see

~~~

January 14

Disciples of Christ

*Come, ye children, hearken unto me;
I will teach you the fear of the Lord.*
Psalm 34:11 (KJV)

Teach me thy word, oh Lord, I pray
That I might tell others of thee
That they might become disciples of Christ
From the punishment of sin set free

January 15

Jesus Carries Me

The Lord is my light and my salvation;
whom shall I fear?
The Lord is the strength of my life;
of whom shall I be afraid? (KJV)
Psalm 27:1

When I am lonely and afraid of life
My soul feels void of light
Jesus lifts and comforts me
And carries me through the night

~~~

January 16

That Which Saves Our Souls

But God commendeth his love toward us in that,
while we were yet sinners, Christ died for us.
Romans 5:8 (KJV)

It's not our works that save our souls
But Christ at Calvary
He only asks that we believe
His gift to us is free

January 17

Off the Beaten Path

*Now the Lord had said unto Abram, get thee out of
thy country, and from thy kindred, and from thy
father's house, unto a land that I will show thee.*
Genesis 12:1 (KJV)

When God has led you off your path
And shown you a need today
Don't be afraid—though it seems impossible
He'll always provide the way

~~~

January 18

Spiritually Minded

*For to be carnally minded is death,
but to be spiritually minded is life and peace.*
Romans 8:6 (KJV)

Battle improper thoughts each day
And the things we see and hear
That our sinful nature might be defeated
Allowing the purity of Christ to appear

January 19

My All

*The Lord is my strength and my shield;
my heart trusted in him and I am helped.
Therefore, my heart greatly rejoiceth,
and with my song will I praise him.*
Psalm 28:7 (KJV)

In all that I say and all that I do
To Christ I'll give the praise
He died for me and saved my soul
And I'll worship Him all of my days

~~~

January 20

Just Passing Through

*Thou wilt keep him in perfect peace,
whose mind is stayed on thee,
because he trusteth in thee.*
Isaiah 26:3 (KJV)

A pilgrim I, just passing through
This world and its glory so fleeting
I'm headed home to eternal peace
My Savior I'll soon be meeting

January 21

The Prize

Know ye not that they who run in a race run all, but one receiveth the prize? So run, that ye may obtain.
1 Corinthians 9:24 (KJV)

Lord give me the strength to go the distance
And keep my faith to the end
That I may hear, when I'm in your presence
Well done my servant and friend

~~~

January 22

Under the Shadow of Your Wings

*Keep me as the apple of the eye;
hide me under the shadow of thy wings.*
Psalm 17:8 (KJV)

Lord keep me close and protect me always
Under the shadow of your wings
Give me the quiet and peaceful assurance
That trust in your promises brings

January 23

At Calvary

*And when they were come to the place,
which is called Calvary, there they crucified him,
and the malefactors, one on the right hand,
and the other on the left.*
Luke 23:33 (KJV)

Christ's cross at Calvary was simply wood
But His blood made it so much more
His death that day covered all our sins
As the temple curtain tore

~~~

January 24

Chiseled

*And be not conformed to this world: but be ye
transformed by the renewing of your mind,
that ye may prove what is that good, and
acceptable, and perfect, will of God.*
Romans 12:2 (KJV)

Lord, as you chisel away my flaws
Make me beautiful in your sight
That I might serve and worship you
Surrounded by your light

January 25

Strengthened and Prepared

*My brethren, count it all joy when ye fall into
various trials, knowing this,
that the testing of your faith worketh patience.*
James 1:2-3 (KJV)

God held my hand when He led me through
Deep waters of peril and strife
He strengthened me and prepared my soul
For future lessons in life

~~~

January 26

Wisdom for Living

*A wise man will hear, and will increase learning;
and a man of understanding
shall attain unto wise counsels.*
Proverbs 1:5 (KJV)

I ask my Lord for wisdom to live
And He answered in a liberal way
I trust in Him to prepare my path
And guide me day by day

January 27

Only a Few Days

*So teach us to number our days, that we
may apply our hearts unto wisdom.*
Psalm 90:12 (KJV)

Life is fleeting like a vapor in time
The days we have are few
So whisper a prayer and finish the tasks
The Spirit has urged you to do

~~~

January 28

Anointed for His Work

*Do not neglect your gift, which was given you
through the prophecy when the body of elders
laid their hands on you.*
1 Timothy 4:14 (NIV)

The Lord has anointed each one of us
To fill a special need
So discover your gift and experience the joy
As you let the spirit lead

January 29

Unsaved

*And ye shall seek me, and find me,
when ye shall search for me with all your heart.*
Jeremiah 29:13 (KJV)

Always searching, ever seeking
Never quite reaching the goal
Continually trying to fill the yearning
That burns within my soul

~~~

January 30

Saved

For to me to live is Christ, and to die is gain.
Philippians 1:21 (KJV)

To God who chose to save my soul
Goes all honor and glory and praise
He has my eternal home prepared
When I reach the end of my days

January 31

God-given Gifts

*We have different gifts,
according to the grace given to each of us.*
Romans 12:6a (KJV)

Our gifts are unique, given by God
For the Body of Christ and His plan
Discover yours—through the Holy Spirit
And do whatever you can

~~~

February 1

Answer His Call

*Behold, I stand at the door and knock;
if any man hear my voice, and open the door,
I will come in to him and will sup with him,
and he with me.*
Revelation 3:20 (KJV)

When Jesus knocks on the door of our hearts
He brings a gift for all
The Holy Spirit is lovingly given
To those who answer His call

February 2

Truths Revealed

For the word of God is living, and powerful, and sharper than any two edged sword, piercing even to the dividing asunder of soul and spirit, and of the joints and marrow, and is a discerner of the thoughts and intents of the heart.
Hebrews 4:12 (KJV)

The more I study the word of the Lord
And hide it in my heart
The more the spirit reveals the truths
That set all Christians apart

February 3

Quiet Time

Thy word have I hidden in mine heart, that I might not sin against thee.
Psalm 119:11 (KJV)

The quiet times I spend with Jesus
Sitting at His feet
Strengthens me and guides me through
The troubles that I meet

February 4

What We Need to Know

He shall cover thee with his feathers,
and under his wings shalt thou trust;
his truth shall be thy shield and buckler.
Psalm 91:4 (KJV)

The spiritual truths we need to know
Are revealed by the Holy Spirit
Given by God in His Holy Word
To those who yearn to hear it

~~~

February 5

His Direction

He is the rock, his work is perfect;
for all his ways are justice;
a God of truth and without iniquity,
just and right is he.
Deuteronomy 32:4 (KJV)

I praise you Lord for who you are
The rock of my salvation
You strengthen me and direct my path
To my heavenly destination

February 6

One Lost Sheep

All we like sheep have gone astray;
we have turned everyone to his own way,
and the Lord hath laid on him the iniquity of us all.
Isaiah 53:6 (KJV)

Heaven rejoices when one lost sheep
Is found and brought to the fowl
Forever forgiven, a child of the King
Is this truly repentant soul

~~~

February 7

Inner Peace

Acquaint now thyself with him and be at peace;
thereby good shall come unto thee.
Job 22:21 (KJV)

Inner peace is never found
In seeking worldly lust
It comes from doing the will of God
In Him you can place your trust

February 8

The Lord's Discipline

*Blessed is the man whom thou chastenest,
O Lord, and teachest him out of thy law.*
Psalm 94:12 (KJV)

Being chastened by the Lord is painful at first
But it shows you are His child
Righteous fruit that submission produces
Makes those days worthwhile

~~~

February 9

We Fall Short

*For all have sinned, and come short of the glory of
God, being justified freely by his grace through the
redemption that is in Christ Jesus.*
Romans 3:23-24 (KJV)

God has said we all fall short
And would suffer eternal loss
But He sent His Son—the perfect one
To die for our sins on the cross

February 10

The Salvation Story

I will bless the Lord at all times;
his praise shall continually be in my mouth.
Psalm 34:1 (KJV)

To God our creator and submissive Savior
Goes all honor and praise and glory
His death on the cross and resurrection
Proclaimed the salvation story

~~~

February 11

God Is Waiting

Precious in the sight of the Lord
is the death of his saints.
Psalm 116:15 (KJV)

What a joy for all to know
As we struggle for one last breath
That God is waiting to take us home
He's already conquered death

February 12

Here to Serve

*If any man serve me, let him follow me;
and where I am, there shall also my servant be:
if any man serve me, him will my father honor.*
John 12:26 (KJV)

We often work to obtain the things
The world says we deserve
But God has said He'll provide for us
He put us here to serve

~~~

February 13

Grace for Each Day

*Moreover, the law entered,
that the offense might abound.
But where sin abounded,
grace did much more abound.*
Romans 5:20 (KJV)

Father, I seek your grace each day
To cover the sins I confess
Strengthen my spiritual walk with you
That I might displease you less

February 14

He Knows Me

But the very hairs of your head are all numbered.
Matthew 10:30 (KJV)

I'm awed to think that Jesus knows
Each tiny hair on my head
And blotted out my sins on the cross
When He died for me instead

~~~

February 15

No Greater Love

*And when they were come to the place
which is called Calvary, there they crucified him,
and the malefactors, one on the right hand
and the other on the left.*
Luke 23:33 (KJV)

No greater love was shown to man
Than Christ at Calvary
He placed our sins upon Himself
When He died for you and me

February 16

Enter In

*Behold, I stand at the door, and knock;
if any man hear my voice, and open the door,
I will come in to him, and sup with him,
and he with me.*
Revelation 3:20 (KJV)

Jesus Christ, the great I am
Is the gate of salvation for all
By faith we have to enter in
To answer His waiting call

~~~

February 17

He Prepares My Place

*In my Father's house are many mansions;
if it were not so, I would have told you.
I go to prepare a place for you.*
John 14:2 (KJV)

I envision my Savior in heaven
Preparing a place for me
Someday I'll go to be with Him
His glorious face I'll see

February 18

Hold My Tongue

*Keep thy tongue from evil,
and thy lips from speaking guile.*
Psalm 34:13 (KJV)

Lord give me the wisdom to hold my tongue
When others around me fail
And allow the calm spirit of understanding
To enter and prevail

February 19

Bear Each Other's Burdens

*Bear ye one another's burdens,
and so fulfill the law of Christ.*
Galatians 6:2 (KJV)

Give me the heart, oh Lord I pray
To rejoice when others succeed
And weep with them when sorrow enters
Use me to meet their need

February 20

His Tasks for Us

*Let us, therefore, come boldly unto
the throne of grace,
that we may obtain mercy,
and find grace to help in time of need.*
Hebrews 4:16 (KJV)

Sometimes the tasks we have to face
Seem hopeless and out of reach
But God takes these and uses them
To get our attention and teach

~~~

February 21

Like Jesus Sees

*But the Lord said to Samuel, look not on his
countenance, nor on the height of his stature,
because I have refused him; for the Lord sees not as
man sees; for man looks on the outward
appearance, but the Lord looks on the heart.*
1 Samuel 16:7 (KJV)

We often judge others from outward appearance
Instead of what's in their heart
Give us the eyes to see like Jesus
What truly sets them apart

February 22

Before We Cast the First Stone

How can you say to your brother, "Brother, let me remove the speck that is in your eye," when you yourself do not see the plank that is in your own eye? Hypocrite! First remove the plank from your own eye, and then you will see clearly to remove the speck from your brother's eye.
Luke 6:42 (NKJV)

The wrongful things others do
Often mirror our own
Help us to pray and confess our sins
Before we cast the first stone

~~~

February 23

Your Word Leads

*Thy word is a lamp unto my feet,
and a light unto my path.*
Psalm 119:105 (KJV)

Your word is like a lamp in the darkness
As I travel along the way
Lead me in a righteous path
That I might never stray

February 24

Thankfulness Reflected

*Enter into his gates with thanksgiving
and unto his courts with praise,
be thankful unto him,
and bless his name.*
Psalm 100:4 (KJV)

Help us, oh Lord, to be thankful each day
Let it reflect in our behavior
The gifts of goodness, mercy and truth
That you gave through our risen Savior

~~~

February 25

All Eyes on Him

*Watch, therefore; for ye know not
what hour your Lord doth come.*
Matthew 24:42 (KJV)

Someday the rich and poor alike
Will see this world grow dim
When our Savior returns in brilliant glory
All eyes will be on Him

February 26

The Vastness of His Glory

*In the beginning God created
the heaven and the earth.*
Genesis 1:1 (KJV)

Our finite minds can't comprehend
The vastness of His glory
Nor grasp the endless love displayed
In God's creation story

~~~

February 27

Empty Yourself

*For whosoever will save his life shall lose it; and
whosoever will lose his life for my sake shall find it.*
Matthew 16:25 (KJV)

To truly become a useful vessel
You must empty yourself
Allowing God to fill you again
With abundant spiritual wealth

February 28

Standing Tall

*Nevertheless, I am continually with thee;
thou hast held me by my right hand.
Thou shalt guide me with thy counsel,
and afterward receive me to glory.
Whom have I in heaven but thee? And there is none
upon earth that I desire beside thee.*
Psalm 73: 23-25 (KJV)

The trials of life often lead me
Where I would stumble and fall
But God continually holds my hand
And keeps me standing tall

~~~

March 1

Open My Eyes

*My earnest expectation and hope is that
Christ will be magnified in my body
whether by life or by death.*
Philippians 1:20 (KJV)

Cover me today with your love, oh Lord,
Draw me closer to thee
Open my eyes to the things eternal
Let others see you in me

March 2

Hear My Cry

*Out of the depths I cry to you,
oh Lord, hear my voice.
Let your ears be attentive to my cry for mercy.*
Psalm 130:1-2 (NIV)

Hear my prayer, oh Lord, I pray
Turn your ear to my plea
Hear the cry of a confessing sinner
And let your grace flow over me

~~~

March 3

Abide with Him

*For God so loved the world that he gave his only
begotten son, that whosoever believeth on him
would not perish but have everlasting life.*
John 3:16 (KJV)

Our earthly wisdom can never fathom
The span of eternity
But abiding there with my loving Savior
Is where I want to be

March 4

The Incarnation

*For unto you is born this day in the city of
David a savior, who is Christ the Lord.*
Luke 2:11 (KJV)

Hallelujah, a Savior is born
God in the form of man
Bringing salvation and endless love
Fulfilling His gospel plan

~~~

March 5

Your Son

*Who is the image of the invisible God,
the first-born of all creation.*
Colossians 1:15 (KJV)

*Jesus said unto him,
"I am the way, the truth, and the life;
no man comes to the Father except through me."*
John 14:6 (NKJV)

Father, we thank you for sending your Son
Your presence made visible to all
Revealing the truth and way to salvation
For all who will answer your call

March 6

God's Gifts

If any man speak, let him speak as the oracles of God . . . that in all things God may be glorified.
1 Peter 4:11 (KJV)

Thank you Lord for the gifts you've given
Let others see Jesus in me
That I would not be magnified
But all the glory to thee

~~~

March 7

No Worries

*Cease from anger, and forsake wrath;
do not fret, it only causes harm.*
Psalm 37:8 (NKJV)

Some actions of others, beyond our control
Produce feelings of anger and hate
Lord, give me the strength to lift them to you
And the courage to patiently wait

March 8

A Rich Man

Because thou sayest, I am rich, and increased with goods, and have need of nothing, and knowest not that thou are wretched, and miserable, and poor, and blind, and naked.
Revelation 3:17 (KJV)

The poorest people rely only on money
Ever fearful their wealth will unfurl
But those who have what Jesus can give
Are the wealthiest in the world

~~~

March 9

Intercessors

Confess your faults one to another and pray for one another, that ye may be healed. The effectual, fervent prayer of a righteous man availeth much.
James 5:16 (KJV)

Be the one who comes to mind
When others think of prayer
To lift them up before the Lord
And show them that you care

March 10

Thou Art with Me

*Yea, though I walk through the valley of the shadow
of death, I will fear no evil; for thou art with me;
thy rod and thy staff they comfort me.*
Psalm 23:4 (KJV)

My walk with the Savior is special now
He keeps me close by His side
Faithfully headed toward His kingdom
Forever with Him to abide

~~~

March 11

The Bread of Life

*And as they were eating, Jesus took bread, blessed
and broke it, and gave it to the disciples.*
Matthew 26:26a (KJV)

You are the bread of life, oh Lord
Sent to the world to save
Help us partake and receive your love
And be thankful for what you gave

March 12

Confession & Cleansing

*If we confess our sins, he is faithful and just to
forgive our sins and to cleanse us
from all unrighteousness.*
1 John 1:9 (KJV)

Cleanse me, oh Lord, with your forgiving power
Help me to not hide my sin
Give me the strength to confess and repent
Let your righteous healing begin

~~~

March 13

Unselfish Ways

*Let nothing be done through strife or vainglory;
but in lowliness of mind let each
esteem others better than themselves.*
Philippians 2:3 (KJV)

Help me serve others before myself
Take all selfish thoughts away
That others might see the example of Jesus
In all that I do each day

March 14

The Value of a Friend

Iron sharpened iron;
so a man sharpened the countenance of his friend.
Proverbs 27:17 (KJV)

Help me always be a friend
To those who count on me
To lift them up and strengthen them
As I would want to be

~~~

March 15

You Are with Me

When you pass through the waters,
I will be with you, and pass through the rivers,
they will not sweep over you.
Isaiah 43:2-3 (NIV)

Lord, help me remember, throughout my life
That everything passes through you
And whatever trials come my way
You'll safely guide me through

March 16

My Refuge

*He is my loving God and my fortress,
my stronghold and my deliverer,
my shield in whom I take refuge.*
Psalm 144:2 (NIV)

You are my God, the great I Am
I praise you with all of my breath
You hide me within your protective arms
And remove the fear of death

~~~

March 17

In His Image

*So God created man in his own image,
in the image of God he created him;
male and female he created them.*
Genesis 1:27 (NIV)

In your image you created us
And gave dominion over things of the earth
When sin crept in, you loved us still
As shown by Jesus' birth

March 18

The Truth of Your Promise

*And, lo, I am with you always,
even unto the end of the age.*
Matt. 28:20b (KJV)

Your promise carries me through each day
Because I know it's true
Your spirit is there to lift me up
Whatever task I do

~~~

March 19

The Value of Wisdom

*For wisdom is better than rubies; and all the things
that may be desired are not to be compared to it.*
Proverbs 7:11 (KJV)

Help me, Father, as I seek you today
Reveal your truths to me
Let me discover your hidden wisdom
And draw me closer to thee

March 20

Empower Me

*And his incomparably great power
for us who believe. That power is like the
working of his mighty strength.*
Ephesians 1:19 (NIV)

Helpless I am to live a righteous life
But you Lord have all the power
Fill me today with your Holy Spirit
Empower me hour by hour

March 21

Filled

*And to know the love of Christ,
which passeth knowledge,
that ye might be filled with all the fullness of God.*
Ephesians 3:19 (KJV)

Thank you Lord for giving to me
Your love so generous and free
Grant me boldness through the Holy Spirit
That I might tell others of thee

March 22

Living Water

*If any man thirst, let him come unto me and drink.
He that believeth on me, as the scripture has said,
out of his heart shall flow rivers of living water.*
John 7:37b-38 (KJV)

Lead me Lord to your living water
And quench my spiritual thirst
By faith I claim your words of promise
And long to be immersed

~~~

March 23

The Baby

*And this will be a sign to you; you will find a Babe
wrapped in swaddling clothes, lying in a manger.*
Luke 2:12 (NKJV)

Born in a manger, His gift to the world
In a town named "house of bread"
This tiny babe became our salvation
Born to rise from the dead

March 24

The Greatest Gift

*And they came with haste, and found Mary, and
Joseph, and the Babe lying in a manger.*
Luke 2:16 (NKJV)

The greatest gift we'll ever receive
A Savior born in the hay
Mary softly whispered "Jesus"
As she tenderly held Him that day

~~~

March 25

My Hope Is You

*For thou art my hope, O Lord God,
thou art my trust from my youth.*
Psalm 71:5 (KJV)

You are my strength and rock of salvation
My trust I have placed in you
Your guidance I seek through the Holy Spirit
In all the things I do

March 26

Acceptable in Your Sight

*Let the words of my mouth and the
meditations of my heart be acceptable in your sight,
O Lord, my strength and my redeemer.*
Psalm 19:14 (KJV)

Our spiritual nourishment is found in your word
Feed me, oh Lord, today
That I might grow strong and reflect your truths
In all that I do and say

~~~

March 27

God's Word for Us

*Let the word of Christ dwell in you richly,
in all wisdom; teaching and
admonishing one another . . .*
Colossians 3:16 (KJV)

We have the word, inspired by God
Given to guide our way
'Tis for us to read and learn
That we might grow each day

March 28

Beneath Your Wings

*Keep me as the apple of thy eye;
hide me under the shadow of thy wings.*
Psalm 17:8 (KJV)

Give me, oh father, a childlike faith
Allow me to rest in you
Hold me close beneath your wings
And whisper what I should do

~~~

March 29

Lord of Lords

*Therefore let all the house of Israel know assuredly,
that God has made that same Jesus, whom ye have
crucified, both Lord and Christ.*
Acts 2:36 (KJV)

Jesus Christ is Lord of Lords
Forever He will reign
For all who choose to follow Him
Eternal life they'll gain

March 30

God's Order

*In the beginning God created
the heaven and the earth.*
Genesis 1:1 (KJV)

The order we see in the universe
Began with the creation story
God's perfect plan, including man
Reflected His power and glory

~~~

March 31

A Helper for Us

*I will pray to the father,
and he shall give you another helper,
that he may abide with you forever.*
John 14:16 (KJV)

The Holy Spirit dwells within us
A helper for sinners set free
Sent by God to those who know Jesus
He's part of the one in three

April 1

A Prepared Place

Let not your hearts be troubled;
ye believe in God, believe also in me.
In my Father's house are many mansions:
if it were not so I would not have told you.
I go to prepare a place for you.
John 14:1-2 (KJV)

When all too soon a loved one's gone
And our eyes are blinded with tears
God's comforting Spirit eases our pain
And calms our many fears

~~~

April 2

Boundless Love

For all have sinned and
come short of the glory of God;
Being justified freely through
the redemption that is in Christ Jesus.
Romans 3:23-24 (KJV)

The price for sin was paid for us
That day on Calvary's tree
Boundless love so undeserved
'Twas grace that set us free

April 3

Omnipotent God

*In the beginning God created
the heaven and the earth.*
Genesis 1:1 (KJV)

The Lord my God is omnipotent
His power is ceaseless and great
The universe is His creation
And nothing is early or late

~~~

April 4

Fearfully and Wonderfully Made

*I will praise you,
for I am fearfully and wonderfully made.*
Psalm 139:14 (NKJV)

Created by God in a special way
Fearfully and wonderfully made
He saw my days from beginning to end
As His perfect plan was laid

April 5

Wisdom Given

If any of you lacks wisdom, let him ask of God, who gives to all liberally and without reproach.
James 1:5a (NKJV)

Come to God and ask in faith
Believing His word is true
And liberal amounts of useful wisdom
Will be given unto you

~~~

April 6

The Price of Salvation

I am the living bread that came down from heaven: if any man eat of this bread he shall live forever; and the bread that I give is my flesh, which I shall give for the life of the world.
John 6:51 (KJV)

Bless me, oh Lord, empower me today
That others might listen and see
Our price for salvation was death on the cross
And has already been paid by thee

April 7

Conviction by the Spirit

*And when He has come, He will convict the world
of sin, and of righteousness, and of judgment.*
John 16:8 (NKJV)

The Holy Spirit convicts the ones
Whose souls are lost to sin
That Jesus may come and offer forgiveness
And cleanse them from within

~~~

April 8

Critical Confession

*If we confess our sins,
he is faithful and just to forgive us our sins,
and to cleanse us of all unrighteousness.*
1 John 1:9 (KJV)

Lord, teach me to pray that I might receive
The blessings you bestow
Help me confess my every sin
And allow your grace to flow

April 9

The Path of a Child

*Train up a child in the way he should go:
and when he is old, he will not depart from it.*
Proverbs 22:6 (KJV)

The things we do our children see
And will often imitate
Guide them early on a godly path
Don't wait until it's too late

~~~

April 10

The Other Things

*Seek ye first the kingdom of God;
and all these things shall be added unto you.*
Luke 12:31 (KJV)

The years I've lived have been wondrous indeed
The lessons I've learned from the past
Happiness is found in Christ alone
All other things don't last

April 11

Sowing and Reaping

Do not be deceived, God is not mocked;
for whatever a man sows, that he will also reap.
Galatians 6:7 (NKJV)

God has said, we cannot hide
The things each day we sow
So carefully plant through the Holy Spirit
And joyfully watch them grow

~~~

April 12

The Gift of Grace

For by grace are ye saved through faith;
and that not of yourselves, it is the gift of God.
Ephesians 2:8 (KJV)

The grace of God is an endless well
That man cannot exhaust
Jesus came to bring salvation
And He's already paid the cost

April 13

Filter Each Challenge

For all that is in the world, the lust of the flesh,
the lust of the eyes, and the pride of life,
is not of the Father, but is of the world.
1 John 2:16 (KJV)

Being a child of the king doesn't make us immune
To Satan's sly deceit
But filtering each challenge through the Holy Spirit
Will keep us from defeat

~~~

April 14

No Matter What We Face

For the grace of God has appeared,
bringing salvation to all men.
Titus 2:11 (NASB)

God's word, goodness, wrath and love
Are given through His grace
They're all we need to live each day
No matter what we face

April 15

His Beloved Son

*For he received from God the Father
honor and glory,
when there came such a voice
to him from the excellent glory:
"This is my beloved Son,
in whom I am well pleased."*
2 Peter 1:17 (KJV)

The word of God is always true
Sent through His beloved Son
That we might worship before His throne
When our work on earth is done

~~~

April 16

Living Temple

For ye are the temple of the living God.
2 Corinthians 6:16a (KJV)

Wherever we are is where we should worship
Whether corporate or alone and simple
God resides in every Christian
For we are His living temple

April 17

Feed My Sheep

Jesus said to him, "Feed my sheep."
John 21:17b (NKJV)

The Lord delights in all I do
That serves and feeds His sheep
He urges us to do His work
Before it's time to sleep

April 18

God's Creation

*In the beginning God created
the heaven and the earth.*
Genesis 1:1 (KJV)

The creations that astound our earthly senses
Either in the heavens or here on earthly sod
Are simply providing a majestic finger
Pointing toward our God

April 19

Our Best

Commit thy way unto the Lord; trust also in him, and he shall bring it to pass.
Psalm 37:5 (KJV)

Anything less than our very best
Is not what the Lord wants to see
He answered the call and gave us His all
That day on Calvary's tree

~~~

April 20

A Humble Servant

Humble yourselves in the sight of the Lord, and he shall lift you up.
James 4:10 (KJV)

Humble me Lord that I may be
A servant like your Son
That when you finally call me home
I'll hear you say "well done"

April 21

He Will Direct

*In all your ways acknowledge Him,
and He shall direct your paths.*
Proverbs 3:6 (NKJV)

Rest your fears upon the Lord
And He will direct thy ways
Trust in Him with all your heart
He'll guide you through life's maze

~~~

April 22

Sacrificial Love

*In this is love, not that we loved God,
but that he loved us and sent his Son
to be the propitiation for our sins.*
1 John 4:10 (KJV)

The greatest love we've ever known
Is not an earthly one
But came in the form of a sacrifice
Our cross was taken by God's Son

April 23

Guiding Wisdom

As for God, His way is perfect; the word of the Lord is proved, he is a shield to all those who trust Him.
Psalm 18:30 (NKJV)

The word of God provides warning signs
That keep us out of harm's way
We need to seek His guiding wisdom
And spend time with Him each day

~~~

April 24

Be Ready

Therefore be ye also ready: for in such an hour as ye think not the Son of man cometh.
Matthew 24:44 (KJV)

We know not the day or the hour He'll come
But we should prepare as if it's today
For He has promised to return again
In a glorious and unexpected way

April 25

The Good Samaritan

*And went to him and bound up his wounds,
pouring in oil and wine
and set him on his own beast,
and brought him to an inn, and took care of him.*
Luke 11:34 (KJV)

Guide me today by the Holy Spirit
Help me to follow, not lead
Prepare me always to be ready for service
To others around me in need

～～～

April 26

Our Reflection

*But we all, with unveiled face,
beholding as in a mirror,
the glory of the Lord,
are being transformed.*
2 Corinthians 3:18a (NKJV)

Lord help me reflect your majestic glory
That others might clearly see
The way to the cross and your priceless gift
That atoned and set us free

April 27

His Yoke

Take my yoke upon you and learn from me,
for I am gentle and humble in heart,
and you will find rest in your souls.
Matthew 11:29 (NKJV)

Give me your yoke, oh Heavenly Father
Lead me in the ways I should go
Teach me to follow your guiding hand
As I continue to learn and grow

~~~

April 28

Take Courage

But Jesus immediately said to them:
"Take courage! It is I. Don't be afraid."
Matthew 13:27 (NIV)

When I am in trials of deep despair
Help me be able to see
That Jesus is walking by my side
And is always there for me

April 29

Renouncing Sin

*Whoever conceals their sins does not prosper,
but the one who confesses and
renounces them finds mercy.*
Proverbs 28:13 (NIV)

Once I was lost, wandering in darkness
And then I heeded His call
Renounced my yearning for worldly pleasures
For He is my all in all

~~~

April 30

Faith Will See You Through

*Now faith is the substance of things hoped for,
the evidence of things not seen.*
Hebrews 11:1 (NKJV)

Always give your very best
For whatever task you do
God will provide your every need
And faith will see you through

May 1

A Worthy Wife

A wife of noble character who can find?
She is worth far more than rubies.
Proverbs 31:10 (NIV)

A marvelous gift bestowed on man
Given by the Lord for life
Nothing compares in a Christian home
To a loving, God fearing wife

~~~

May 2

To Follow the Lord

Commit your way to the Lord, trust also in him,
and he shall bring it to pass.
Psalm 37:5 (KJV)

Guide my steps, oh Heavenly Father
Give me the strength today
To seek your will and not my own
As I follow you along the way

May 3

Covenant Marriage

*Yet she is your companion and
your wife by covenant.*
Malachi 2:14 (NKJV)

What a wonderful feeling to know we are one
A covenant bond with my wife
An institution created by God
Ordained to last for life

~~~

May 4

Closer to Him

Be still and know that I am God.
Psalm 46:10 (NKJV)

The quiet time I spend with Jesus
Brings me closer to Him
He strengthens me for daily warfare
In this world of continuous sin

May 5

Christ's Love

To know the love of Christ which passes knowledge;
that you may be filled with all the fullness of God.
Ephesians 3:19 (NKJV)

To explain the love of God is beyond our comprehension
To grasp the scope of it is simply beyond our power
It remains for us to appreciate this love as we expand our knowledge of Him
Knowing we'll never experience its fullness until our final hour

~~~

May 6

Sweet Rest

He said to them, "Come with me by yourselves
to a quiet place and get some rest."
Mark 6:31b (NIV)

Jesus is where I find sweet rest
From the toils and troubles of the day
He invites me in to fellowship with Him
Then directs me on my way

May 7

Faith Like a Mustard Seed

Verily I say unto you, If you have faith as a grain of mustard seed, ye shall say unto this mountain, move from here to yonder place; and it shall move; and nothing shall be impossible to you.
Matthew 17:20 (KJV)

Striving to live by faith today
Will strengthen our walk for tomorrow
God is there and will meet our needs
Through joy, pain and sorrow

~~~

May 8

Turn from Idols

*Thus says the Lord God,
"Repent, turn away from your idols,
and turn your faces away from
all your abominations."*
Ezekiel 14:6 (KJV)

Help me Lord to remove all idols
From your throne that resides in me
That you alone would be there seated
And I would worship only thee

May 9

By Faith

But without faith it is impossible to please him.
Hebrews 11:6 (KJV)

Live today as though you know
That Jesus is coming tomorrow
Live by faith and look ahead
Forget past sins and sorrow

May 10

The Holy Spirit's Voice

For He Himself has said,
"I will never leave you nor forsake you."
So we may boldly say,
"The Lord is my helper, I will not fear."
Hebrews 13:5-6 (NKJV)

The still small voice of the Holy Spirit
Quiets my fears when they call
He fills that lonely, frightful void
That appears within us all

May 11

Keep Us Lord

Have mercy on me, O Lord, for I am weak;
O Lord, heal me, for my bones are troubled.
Psalm 6:2 (NKJV)

God will keep us and meet our needs
In our journeys wherever we fare
He's there to give us His loving grace
If we seek Him in earnest prayer

~~~

May 12

Like Abraham Trusted

And Abraham said,
"My son, God will provide Himself a lamb
for a burnt offering;
so they went both of them together.
Genesis 22:8 (NKJV)

Faith in God will see us through
Like Abraham on the mountain
Trust in Him for everything
And blessings will flow like a fountain

May 13

More Like Jesus

He who has begun a good work in you will
perform it until the day of Jesus Christ.
Philippians 1:6 (NKJV)

Do not observe the faults in me
For His work in me is not done
The Lord is changing me day by day
Making me more and more like His Son

May 14

Faith Is . . .

Now faith is the substance of things hoped for,
the evidence of things not seen.
Hebrews 11:1 (NKJV)

Faith is not an empty vessel
That must be filled to the rim
It's simply believing what God has said
And putting our trust in Him

May 15

Body Temple

*Do you not know that your body is the temple of the
Holy Spirit who is in you, whom you have from
God, and you are not your own?*
1 Corinthians 6:19 (NASB)

Lord, cleanse my body and mind of things
That harm my fellowship with thee
Fill me today with the Holy Spirit
That others might see Jesus in me

~~~

May 16

Spirit Intercedes

*The Spirit Himself makes intercession for us
with groanings which cannot be uttered.*
Romans 8:26b (NKJV)

When I am distraught and cannot pray
God's spirit hears my mutter
He prays for me within God's will
For things I cannot utter

May 17

Follow His Path

We must obey God rather than men.
Acts 5:29 (NASB)

Help me to know which path to follow
In daily choices I make
Guide me by the Holy Spirit
On every journey I take

May 18

The Word as Warning

*These things happened to them as examples,
and they were written for our admonition.*
1 Corinthians 10:11 (NKJV)

Lord, your word is there to keep us safe
To warn us of our sin
Help us to hide it in our hearts
So we don't go where others have been

May 19

Redeemed by Christ

That he no longer should live the rest of his time in the flesh for the lusts of men, but for the will of God.
1 Peter 4:2 (NKJV)

When I selfishly use my time on earth
I'm reminded it's not mine to give
The debt I owed was redeemed by Christ
His sacrifice allowed me to live

~~~

May 20

You Are There

Where can I go from Your Spirit?
Or where can I flee from Your presence?
Psalm 139:7 (NASB)

You are there Lord; you are there
Wherever I wander, whenever I pray
You are there Lord; you are there
Whenever I cry out, you show me the way

May 21

Upon That Cross

*When Jesus, therefore, had received the vinegar,
he said, "It is finished";
and he bowed his head and gave up the Spirit.*
John 19:30 (NKJV)

Upon that cross in agony and sorrow
No light in which to see
Jesus died as the Lamb of God
A sacrifice for you and me

~~~

May 22

He Rose Victorious

*For God so loved the world
that he gave his only begotten son,
that whosoever believeth in him
should not perish but have everlasting life.*
John 3:16 (KJV)

Why would Jesus do such a thing for me
Dying on the cross to set my soul free
Empowered by His Father in heaven above
He rose victorious; He did it all in love

May 23

Endless Love

*And we have known and believed the love
that God has for us. God is love,
and he who dwells in love,
dwells in God, and God in him.*
1 John 4:16 (NKJV)

Only a God with endless love
Can lift me again when I fall
Only He deserves the glory
His love explains it all

May 24

Restoring Beauty

*And I will restore to you the years
that the swarming locust has eaten.*
Joel 2:25 (NKJV)

Destructive living in years gone past
That created misery and strife
Can be restored by our Heavenly Father
And give us back a beautiful life

May 25

The Prize Winner

*Do you not know that those who run
in a race all run,
but one receives the prize.*
1 Corinthians 9:24 (NASB)

When we run the race for worldly prizes
Time destroys them whatever we do
Our works for God receive heavenly treasures
So run the race with eternity in view

~~~

May 26

The Believer's Defense

Sanctify them through thy truth; thy word is truth.
John 17:17 (KJV)

Daily reading of the word of God
Is the defense for every believer
By following His truths through the Holy Spirit
We can ward off the great deceiver

May 27

That Glorious Day

Say to those who are fearful hearted,
"Be strong, do not fear!
Behold your God will come with vengeance,
with the recompense of God;
He will come and save you."
Isaiah 35:4 (NKJV)

Pain and suffering, regrets and guilt
Daily they invade our lives
But all will be gone on that glorious day
When our redeeming Savior arrives

~~~

May 28

Gracious Provision

For we brought nothing into this world,
and it is certain we can carry nothing out.
1 Timothy 6:7 (KJV)

Lord keep me content with your gracious provisions
May my witness be pure and bold
May I never lose sight of your cross of salvation
Or fall prey to a god of gold

May 29

Empowered Speech

*Then Philip opened his mouth,
and beginning at this scripture,
preached Jesus to him.*
Acts 8:35 (NKJV)

Lord, strengthen us today wherever we are
To reveal to someone your Son
Empower our speech through the Holy Spirit
To tell others one by one

~~~

May 30

Press On

*I press toward the mark for the prize
of the high calling of God in Christ Jesus.*
Philippians 3:14 (NKJV)

'Tis God, my Father, I'll always choose
All the world offers, mine to refuse
Confident and steady in this race that I run
Straining for the prize of hearing "well done my faithful son"

May 31

Things Not Seen

*While we look not at the things which are seen,
but at the things which are not seen:
for the things which are seen are temporal,
but the things which are not seen are eternal.*
2 Corinthians 4:18 (KJV)

Guard me from the fleeting pleasures
The sinful world displays
Keep my eyes on eternal prizes
That await at the end of my days

~~~

June 1

Count It as Gain

*Choosing rather to suffer affliction
with the people of God than to enjoy
the pleasures of sin for a season.*
Hebrews 11:25 (KJV)

Living for Christ will certainly bring
Reproach from the world as its cost
But my faith comes from the righteous Lord
And I count it as gain not loss

June 2

Simply Believe

Where is boasting then? It is excluded.
By what law? Of works?
Nay: but by the law of faith.
Romans 3:27 (KJV)

God's provision for getting to heaven
Is simple and does not deceive
The world says works will get you there
But God says simply believe

~~~

June 3

A Suitable Helper

The Lord God said,
"It is not good for man to be alone,
I will make a helper suitable for him."
Genesis 2:18 (NIV)

God gave man a wonderful gift
To share this earthly life
A helper, a lover, an intimate friend
This person we call a wife

June 4

His Rest

*Come to me,
all you who labor and are heavy laden,
and I will give you rest.*
Matthew 11:28 (NKJV)

Jesus is calling for all to come home
Home to His rest and peace
To accept His gift of eternal salvation
Where your burdens you can finally release

~~~

June 5

With Us

*Lo, I am with you always,
even to the end of the age.*
Matthew 28:20 (NKJV)

The Lord is with us all the time
In light and dark of night
An unseen presence to meet our needs
We're always in His sight

June 6

Whatever You Do

*Whatever you do in word or deed,
do all in the name of Lord Jesus.*
Colossians 3:17 (NKJV)

Many of our tasks in the eyes of the world
Are nothing for which we should boast
But do them all in the name of the Lord
The One who should matter the most

~~~

June 7

Our Shepherd

*For thus says the Lord God:
"Indeed I Myself will
search for My sheep and seek them out."*
Ezekiel 34:11 (NKJV)

Jesus Christ, the Lamb of God
Died on Calvary to set us free
Now He reigns as our promised shepherd
And daily watches over you and me

June 8

Troubled Times

*For he commands and raises the stormy wind,
which lifts up waves of the sea.*
Psalm 107: 25 (NKJV)

When troubled times are heaped upon you
And life has loaded your plate
Turn those storms over to the Lord
He will teach you how to navigate

~~~

June 9

Doers of the Word

*Be doers of the word and not hearers only,
deceiving yourselves.*
James 1:22 (NKJV)

We must do more than read His word
To cope with things we do
We must be doers and acknowledge Him
And His love will see us through

June 10

Your Shining Glory

*For to be carnally minded is death,
but to be spiritually minded is life and peace.*
Romans 8:6 (NKJV)

Draw me closer to thee, oh Lord
So your glory will come shining through
Chip away my imperfections
That I might be pleasing to you

~~~

June 11

A Total Commitment

But they first gave themselves to the Lord.
2 Corinthians 8:5b (NKJV)

Most think they owe but just a tenth
From the blessings God freely gives
But a total commitment is what we owe
And is shown by how one lives

June 12

The Necessity of Humility

*But when he was strong, his heart was lifted up,
to his destruction; for he transgressed
against the Lord his God, by entering the temple of
the Lord to burn incense on the altar of incense.*
2 Chronicles 26:16 (NKJV)

The slippery slope of pride is there
It tests us along the way
Our salvation lies in remaining humble
While serving the Lord each day

June 13

See Jesus in Me

*Let the words of my mouth, and
the meditation of my heart,
be acceptable in Your sight,
O Lord, my strength, and my Redeemer.*
Psalm 19:14 (NKJV)

Help me Lord to face each day
By keeping my eyes upon you
That others might see the presence of Jesus
In everything I do

June 14

Does He Care

*Jesus began to be troubled and deeply distressed.
Then he said to them,
"My soul is exceedingly sorrowful even to death."*
Mark 14:33-34 (NKJV)

Days when burdens consume my prayers
I wonder, does He even care or hear
But then I recall when Jesus prayed
He, too, experienced fear

~~~

June 15

Answer His Call

*Now therefore, fear the Lord and
serve Him in sincerity and truth.*
Joshua 24:14a (NKJV)

An ordinary person empowered by God
With gifts to fill a need
Can serve the Lord in unique ways
By answering His call to lead

June 16

Follow You Lord

*For to be carnally minded is death,
but to be spiritually minded is life and peace.*
Romans 8:6 (NKJV)

Teach us Lord to follow you
And not the world we see
For only you can quiet our fears
And truly set us free

~~~

June 17

Teaching Our Children

*And thou shalt teach them diligently unto thy
children, and shalt talk of them when thou sitteth in
thine house, and when thou walketh by the way and
when thou liest down, and when thou riseth up.*
Deuteronomy 6:7 (KJV)

Teach your children to love the Lord
And seek everything in His name
So when they're parents, they will remember these things
And teach their children the same

June 18

He Leads Me

*He restores my soul; He leads me in the paths
of righteousness for His name's sake.*
Psalm 23:3 (NKJV)

Those times when your path seems totally lost
And strife envelopes each day
Relinquish the lead and learn to follow
For Jesus knows the way

~~~

June 19

Sweeter Than Honey

*How sweet are Your words to my taste,
sweeter than honey to my mouth.*
Psalm 119:103 (NKJV)

Fill me with your word, dear Lord
Nourish me as I read
Satisfy my spiritual craving
And meet my every need

June 20

Fill Me Lord

*Watch, stand fast in the faith,
be brave, be strong.*
1 Corinthians 16:13 (NKJV)

Fill me Lord, replace the carnal
That filled my soul at birth
Instill in me the spiritual values
That Jesus taught us on earth

~~~

June 21

Trust and Obey

*Have not I commanded thee?
Be strong and of good courage;
be not afraid, neither be thou dismayed:
for the Lord thy God is
with thee wherever thou goest.*
Joshua 1:9 (KJV)

Wherever the Lord tells me to go
I'll trust in His strength and obey
For I trust in Him to see me through
And lead me along the way

June 22

Do Not Add to the Word

You shall not add to the word which I command you, nor take from it, that you may keep the commandments of the Lord your God.
Deuteronomy 4:2 (NKJV)

God's word needs no addition
Nor should we take away
Strive to live by its guiding principles
And produce a fruitful day

~~~

June 23

Call Me Home

Abraham waited for the city which has foundations, whose builder and maker is God.
Hebrews 11:10 (NKJV)

Help me Lord to remember this world
Is just a stopping place
When you call me home, this journey will end
And I'll meet you face to face

June 24

Redeemed by the Blood

For you know it was not with perishable things such as silver and gold that you were redeemed from the empty way of life handed down to you from your ancestors, but with the precious blood of Christ, as of a lamb without blemish or defect.
1 Peter 1:18-19 (NIV)

Forsaken by God, humiliation and agony
All seen in His tortured face
As Jesus hung on the cross that day
God gave us His ultimate grace

~~~

June 25

Doers of the Word

Prove yourselves doers of the word and not merely hearers who delude themselves.
James 1:22 (NASB)

Reading God's word is what we should do
But it's not a passive plan
We must take action and witness to others
Of where our redemption began

June 26

Bear Fruit

They shall still bear fruit in old age;
they shall be fresh and flourishing.
Psalm 92:14 (NKJV)

Fill my heart today, dear Lord
With love only you can give
That it might flow into other lives
And teach them how to live

~~~

June 27

Sinless and Blameless

He Himself is the propitiation for our sins,
and not for ours only but also for the whole world.
1 John 2:2 (NKJV)

Sinless and blameless He came to this earth
Entering this world by a Virgin's birth
He loved us so much He died one day
Taking our blame and sin away

June 28

The Good Shepherd

*I am the good shepherd and know my sheep,
and am known of mine.*
John 10:14 (KJV)

God often disciplines His children
When we ignore His will and stray
We can heed His warnings and return to the fold
Or expect fatherly action if we dare disobey

~~~

June 29

Forgive Them, Lord

*When they had come to the place called Calvary,
there they crucified him.*
Luke 23:33a (NKJV)

That day at the cross, we were standing there
Our sins had nailed Him to that tree
But Jesus uttered, "Forgive them, Lord"
As He died for you and me

June 30

Keep Your Eyes on the Lord

But if we walk in the light as he is in the light,
we have fellowship with one another,
and the blood of Jesus Christ His Son
cleanses us from all sin.
1 John 1:7 (NKJV)

'Tis no gain to dwell on regrets
For things that occurred in the past
Keep your eyes on the Lord ahead
And you'll build sweet memories that last

~~~

July 1

Shield Me from Evil

The temple of God is holy, which temple you are.
1 Corinthians 3:17b (NKJV)

Strengthen me, Lord, against evil influences
That threaten your temple each day
Shield me from them through the Holy Spirit
Help me to turn them away

July 2

Unselfish Servant

He must increase but I must decrease.
John 3:30 (KJV)

Help me, oh Lord, to be an unselfish servant
Sensitive to others in need
Setting aside my personal ambitions
To follow wherever you lead

July 3

This Is the Way

*And thine ears shall hear
a word behind thee saying,
This is the way, walk ye in it,
when ye turn to the right hand,
and when ye turn to the left.*
Isaiah 30:21 (KJV)

Striving each day to reach the goal
That Jesus has set for all
I pray that His spirit will guide me
That I may not stumble and fall

July 4

Your Infinite Works

O Lord, how manifold are your works!
In wisdom you have made them all.
The earth is full of your possessions.
Psalm 104:24 (NKJV)

Lord, when I observe your vast creation
From early dawn to the setting sun
It's a visual reminder of your magnificent glory
And the infinite works that you have done

~~~

July 5

Faithful Steward

"What do you have that you did not receive?"
1 Corinthians 4:7a (NKJV)

All that I have and all that I give
Is a gift from the Lord above
Entrusted to me as a faithful steward
To be used with prayer and love

July 6

The Lord Is My Help

*I will lift my eyes to the hills—
from whence comes my help?
My help comes from the Lord,
who made heaven and earth.*
Psalm 121:1-2 (NKJV)

The Lord is my help in times of trouble
He hears me when I cry
In Him I put my everlasting trust
To guide me till I die

~~~

July 7

Words of Warning

*Beware, brethren, lest there be any of you an evil
heart of unbelief in departing from the living God.*
Hebrews 3:12 (NKJV)

The warnings in God's word are given to us
To lovingly protect and preserve
That we may receive a fulfilled life
Instead of one we deserve

July 8

No Darkness

*This, then, is the message
which we have heard from Him,
and declare to you, that God is light,
and in Him is no darkness at all.*
1 John 1:5 (NKJV)

Lord, help me to have a yielded spirit
That others might always see
Your heavenly light of forgiving love
Always shining through me

~~~

July 9

Focus Forward

*But I press on, that I may lay hold of that for which
Christ Jesus has also laid hold of me.*
Philippians 3:12b (NKJV)

Keep my eyes focused forward
That I might keep moving ahead
Forgetting the past and all my failures
Draw me closer to Jesus instead

July 10

Learn to Serve

*And whoever of you desires
to be first shall be slave of all.*
Mark 10:44 (NKJV)

Do not seek to be exalted by man
With praise you think you deserve
Jesus said to be first among others
You first must learn how to serve

~~~

July 11

Love Measured

*These people draw near to Me with their mouth,
and honor Me with their lips,
but their heart is far from Me.*
Matthew 15:8 (NKJV)

God does not measure our love for Him
By the words that we may say
But our heart reveals our true desires
By our actions day by day

July 12

Sown Seeds

*Some fell on stony places,
where they did not have much earth;
and they immediately sprang up
because they had no depth of earth.*
Matthew 13:5 (NKJV)

Lord, create in me a fertile heart
So every seed you sow
Might steadily become deeply rooted
And continue to flourish and grow

July 13

Jesus Deserves My Praise

*For ye are bought at a price;
therefore, glorify God in your body,
and in your spirit, which are God's.*
1 Corinthians 6:20 (NKJV)

Paid in blood on Calvary's tree
God's only Son died there for me
He alone deserves my praise
As I strive for Him throughout my days

July 14

He Surrounds Me

Who shall separate us from the love of Christ?
Romans 8:35a (NKJV)

When worldly pleasures have failed my needs
God is always there
Waiting for me with open arms
To surround me with love and care

~~~

July 15

Strength for the Coming Day

To you, O my strength, I will sing praises;
for God is my defense, My God of mercy.
Psalm 59:17 (NKJV)

When night brings thoughts of doubt and fear
And ebbs your confidence away
Just rest in the Lord's abiding love
And receive strength for the coming day

July 16

Comfort Begets Comfort

*And our hope for you is steadfast, because we know
that as you are partakers of the suffering,
so also you will partake of the consolation.*
2 Corinthians 1:7 (NKJV)

We should comfort those who suffer alone
In Christ, they're our sisters and brothers
God sent His spirit to comfort us
So we can comfort others

~~~

July 17

Gifts for Ministry

*As each one has received a gift,
minister it to one another,
as good stewards of the
manifold grace of God.*
1 Peter 4:10 (NKJV)

God has gifted each of us
With abilities for His praise and glory
That we might use them to minister to others
And proclaim His salvation story

July 18

Through a Darkened Glass

*I sought the Lord, and He heard me,
and delivered me from all my fears.*
Psalm 34:4 (NKJV)

Dimly we see through a darkened glass
Through time what the Lord has revealed
But clearly we know by trusting our Savior
Our security of salvation is sealed

~~~

July 19

Faithful in the Little Things

*He who is faithful in a very little thing
is faithful also in much.*
Luke 16:10a (NASB)

Lord, keep me faithful in the little things
That you have entrusted to me
So I might remember in larger ones
That it all belongs to thee

July 20

Do Not Worry about Tomorrow

*Therefore, do not worry about tomorrow,
for tomorrow will worry about its own things.
Sufficient for the day is its own trouble.*
Matthew 6:34 (NKJV)

Keep me focused on present things
When I come to you Lord and pray
Seeking guidance for the things at hand
For tomorrow's another day

July 21

Resist the Devil

*Be sober, be vigilant; because your adversary
the devil walks about like a roaring lion,
seeking whom he may devour.*
1 Peter 5:8 (NKJV)

Be ready to resist the adversary
For he stalks us every hour
Seeking to find our weakest moment
Waiting to pounce and devour

July 22

Winning Souls

*Whatever you do, do your work heartily
as for the Lord rather than for men.*
Colossians 3:23 (NASB)

Lord, keep me always in the game
Not watching from the side
Winning souls for Jesus Christ
Instead of wishing I'd tried

July 23

Walk in the Light

*For you were once darkness,
but now you are light in the Lord.
Walk as children of light.*
Ephesians 5:8 (NKJV)

When my burdens are such that my heart is heavy
And I yearn for the sleep of night
Then I faithfully wait for joy in the morning
That comes when we walk in the light

July 24

Exalted

I tell you this man went down to his house justified rather than the other; for everyone who exalts himself will be humbled, and he who humbles himself will be exalted.
Luke 18:14 (NKJV)

Keep me Lord from arrogant pride
In choices I make each day
May all my thoughts in you abide
In whatever I do or say

July 25

What Comes Tomorrow

Trust in the Lord with all your heart, and lean not on your own understanding; in all your ways acknowledge Him, and He shall direct your paths.
Proverbs 3:5-6 (NKJV)

May I always trust in you, oh Lord
And not follow my own accord
Guide me through times of joy and sorrow
For only you know what comes tomorrow

July 26

Ours Is Not to Question

As for God, His way is perfect,
the word of the Lord is proved;
He is a shield to all those who trust in Him.
Psalm 18:30 (NKJV)

Ours is not to question when
As we seek His will and pray
For He will answer in His time
And in the perfect way

~~~

July 27

A Good Work

Being confident of this very thing,
that he who has begun a good work in you will
perform it until the day of Jesus Christ.
Philippians 1:6 (NKJV)

A bad experience that affects our lives
Is rarely understood
But God, our Father, can take these things
And turn them into good

July 28

We Are His Disciples

*By this all will know that you are My disciples,
if you have love for one another.*
John 13:35 (NKJV)

Love one another, as Christ loves us
Is one of the Lord's commands
That others might see that we are disciples
Giving what love demands

~~~

July 29

Our Great Reward

*After these things the word of the Lord came
unto Abram in a vision saying, "Fear not, Abram:
I am thy shield, and thy exceedingly great reward."*
Genesis 15:1 (KJV)

The treasures of this world are the ultimate goal
For those who don't walk with the Lord
But seeing His face when we awake
Will be our greatest reward

July 30

God Is on Our Side

The Lord is on my side; I will not fear.
Psalm 118:6 (NKJV)

In all the trials we face each day
Seek the One who will provide
He'll welcome you with mercy and love
For God is on our side

July 31

A Way of Escape

No temptation has overtaken you except such as is common to man; but God is faithful, who will not allow you to be tempted beyond what you are able, but with the temptation will also make the way of escape, that you may be able to bear it.
1 Corinthians 10:13 (NKJV)

Run to God when Satan tempts you
With things you've seen or heard
He'll make a way for your escape
Through the power of His cleansing word

August 1

Godly Sorrow

*I rejoice, not that you were made sorry,
but that your sorrow led to repentance.
For you were made sorry in a godly manner.*
2 Corinthians 7:9a (NKJV)

My sins in this world had led to sorrow
But sorrow in a godly manner
Which produced repentance and eternal salvation
I now carry the Christian banner

~~~

August 2

All Your Needs

*My God shall supply all your needs according to
his riches in glory in Jesus Christ.*
Philippians 4:19 (KJV)

Use your blessings to help one another
Not seeking fame or reward
But knowing that God will meet your needs
No one can outgive the Lord

August 3

Hidden Wisdom

*We speak the wisdom of God in a mystery,
the hidden wisdom,
which God ordained before the ages.*
1 Corinthians 2:7 (NKJV)

The only thing we need to know
That truly sets us free
The crucifixion and resurrection of Jesus Christ
He died for you and me

~~~

August 4

With Me Every Hour

*"I will never desert you,
nor will I ever forsake you."*
Hebrews 13:5 (NASB)

He is with me every hour
By my side whatever the task
The Holy Spirit is there to guide me
All I have to do is ask

August 5

Defend Yourself

For there shall arise false Christs,
and false prophets,
and shall show great signs,
and wonders insomuch that,
if it were possible,
they shall deceive the very elect.
Matthew 24:24 (KJV)

When Satan threatens what you believe
With falsehoods you have heard
Defend yourself as Jesus would
By using God's mighty word

~~~

August 6

Light of the World

The entrance of your words gives light;
it gives understanding to the simple.
Psalm 119:130 (NKJV)

Jesus Christ is the light of the world
His word will open your eyes
Revealing His truths that set you free
From Satan's binding lies

August 7

Faith to Do Your Work

*Six days you shall labor and do all your work,
but the seventh is the Sabbath of the Lord your God.*
Exodus 20:9-10a (NKJV)

Lord, give me faith to do your work
And tell your redemption story
How you died on the cross for all our sins
And rose again in glory

~~~

August 8

Truths Revealed

*He shall cover thee with his feathers,
and under his wings shalt thou trust;
his truth shall be thy shield and buckler.*
Psalm 91:4 (KJV)

As the rain nourishes the blooming flowers
May your words be a blessing to me
Reveal your truths in the Holy Scripture
That I might grow as I follow thee

August 9

Beneath Your Wing

Where can I go from your spirit?
Or where can I flee from your presence?
Psalm 139:7 (NKJV)

You lift me up from all despair
I rest my cares in thee
You comfort me beneath your wing
Oh Lord, you set me free

~~~

August 10

Shining Light

Let your light so shine before men that they may see
your works and glorify your father in heaven.
Matthew 5:16 (NKJV)

Let my light shine exceedingly bright
That it may be seen by all men
That others may know that I follow Christ
Our Savior who died for our sin

August 11

Was Jesus Known

*Then he went down with them and came to
Nazareth, and was subject to them,
but His mother kept all these things in her heart.*
Luke 2:51 (NKJV)

Doesn't matter where you grew up
Some places can hardly be found
What really matters is how you grew up
And was Jesus known in that town

~~~

August 12

Step by Step

*The steps of a good man are ordered by the Lord,
and He delights in his way.*
Psalm 37:23 (NKJV)

Step by step I'll follow His path
And do what He directs for today
I'll rest in the comfort that He knows the future
And wait while God shows me the way

August 13

The Beginning of Wisdom

*The fear of the Lord is the beginning of wisdom,
and the knowledge of the
Holy One is understanding.*
Proverbs 9:10 (NKJV)

Guide my paths, Oh Lord, my Savior
Guard me in what I say
Fill me with the Holy Spirit
And give me wisdom I pray

~~~

August 14

Comfort You

*And many of the Jews had joined
the women around Martha and Mary,
to comfort them concerning their brother.*
John 11:19 (NKJV)

May God allow me to comfort you
Whenever you're in pain and grief
For our souls are utterly bound together
During this journey on earth which is brief

August 15

Let Go of Regrets

Forgetting what lies behind and reaching forward to what lies ahead, and press on toward the goal.
Philippians 3:13-14 (NASB)

Help me, Lord, to just let go
Of things I regret in the past
Allowing your Spirit to fill my life
With the spiritual joys that last

~~~

August 16

Daily Walk

Woe to those who call evil good, and good evil.
Isaiah 5:20 (NKJV)

We receive wisdom by reading God's word
And discern what's evil or good
Giving us guidance in our daily walk
To do the things we should

August 17

Guard My Desires

*Put on the whole armor of God,
that you may be able to stand
against the wiles of the devil.*
Ephesians 6:11 (NKJV)

Lord, keep my eyes directly on you
My life to you I give
Guard my desires from worldly things
For you I want to live

~~~

August 18

As I Travel

*The Lord is compassionate and gracious,
slow to anger and abounding in love.*
Psalm 103:8 (NIV)

Help me, Lord, to follow your path
As I work from day to day
Knowing you supply all you demand
As I travel along the way

August 19

The Holy Spirit Guides Me

*The Helper, the Holy Spirit, whom
the Father will send in My name,
He will teach you all things, and bring to your
remembrance all things that I said to you.*
John 14:26 (NKJV)

Guide me, oh Lord, through the Holy Spirit
As I pray to you each day
Make my requests your will for my life
Teach me what I should say

~~~

August 20

The Way, the Truth, and the Life

*Jesus said to him,
"I am the way, the truth, and the life.
No one comes to the father except through Me."*
John 14:6 (NKJV)

Jesus exclaimed for all to hear
"I am the way, the truth, and the life"
He is the One who has conquered death
And helps bear all your burdens and strife

August 21

Share Gifts with Others

*Do not withhold good from those to whom it is due,
when it is in the power of your hands to do so.*
Proverbs 3:27 (NKJV)

God placed in every believer's hands
The tools that equip us to serve
Share with others these heavenly gifts
Don't just stand and observe

~~~

August 22

Empower Me, Lord

*But you will receive power when the Holy Spirit
comes on you; and you will be witnesses in
Jerusalem, and in all Judea and Samaria, and to the
ends of the earth.*
Acts 1:8 (NJKV)

Empower me, Lord, with your Holy Spirit
That my witness might be strong and bold
Give me the passion to share with others
The greatest story ever told

August 23

Resist and Flee

*How then can I do this great wickedness,
and sin against God?*
Genesis 39:9b (NKJV)

The world is full of sinful temptations
We face them every day
But resist and flee, use the truth of His word
The Lord will provide the way

~~~

August 24

When We All Meet in Heaven

*Behold the tabernacle of God is with men,
and He will dwell with them,
and they shall be His people.*
Revelation 21:3 (NKJV)

Oh for the joy when we all meet in heaven
What a day of rejoicing that will be
Eternal blessings with our Heavenly Father
From worldly burdens we'll be set free

August 25

The Invitation

*Let us therefore come boldly to the throne of grace,
that we may obtain mercy and
find grace to help in time of need.*
Hebrews 4:16 (NKJV)

God has invited all believers
To come to His holy place
To voice our burdens through the Holy Spirit
Who lays them at His throne of grace

~~~

August 26

The Gospel Is Power

*The gospel of Christ . . . is the power of God
to salvation for everyone who believes.*
Romans 1:16 (NKJV)

The word of God is filled with power
For everyone who is a believer
It gives us strength to witness each day
As we battle the great deceiver

August 27

Call upon the Lord

In my distress I called upon the Lord,
and cried to my God for help.
Psalm 18:6 (NIV)

Persistent prayer for enduring trials
Is always what we should do
The Lord will answer in His own time
And always see us through

~~~

August 28

Freedom from Sin

If the Lord delights in us,
then he will bring us into this land and give it to us.
Numbers 14:8a (NKJV)

The restrictions of faith we hear from His word
Delivers us from where we've been
It leads us to freedom if we trust and obey
And frees us from the slavery of sin

August 29

Face to Face

*And if I go and prepare a place for you,
I will come again, and receive you unto myself,
that where I am, there ye may be also.*
John 14:3 (KJV)

Praise God from whom all blessings flow
For those who live by grace
Someday when life on earth is done
We'll meet Him face to face

~~~

August 30

Send Me

*I heard the voice of the Lord saying
"Whom shall I send, and who will go for us?"
Then I said, "Here am I; send me."*
Isaiah 6:8 (KJV)

Forgive my sins and cleanse my soul
Prepare my heart and make me bold
Give me the passion to tell about thee
I'll answer the call, Lord, please send me

August 31

Teach Me to Pray

I want the men everywhere to pray.
1 Timothy 2:8 (NIV)

Teach me, oh Lord, to pray today
Give me the words to speak
Fill me and guide me through the Holy Spirit
For it's your will in my life I seek

~~~

September 1

Praise You for Blessings or Trials

*Shall we indeed accept good from God,
and shall we not accept adversity?*
Job 2:10 (NKJV)

Lord, give me the strength to be like Job
When adversity comes my way
Praising you always for blessings or trials
That you bestow on me each day

September 2

Liberty

*Do not use liberty as an opportunity for the flesh,
but through love serve one another.*
Galatians 5:13b (NKJV)

Thank you Lord for your saving grace
Which sets me free to live
Led by your Spirit day by day
I'm learning to love and give

~~~

September 3

The Works God Requires

*Then they asked him,
"What must we do to do the works God requires?"*
John 6:28 (NIV)

Jesus paid the ultimate price
When He died on the cross for us all
We should respond by living by faith
And daily answering His call

September 4

The Joy That Awaits

*Eye has not seen, nor ear heard, nor have entered
into the heart of man the things which
God has prepared for those who love Him.*
1 Corinthians 2:9 (NKJV)

The joy that awaits, prepared by the Lamb
Will flow from His throne of grace
We'll worship and serve and finally meet
Our Savior, face to face

~~~

September 5

Your Righteous Light

*And have no fellowship with the unfruitful works of
darkness, but rather expose them.*
Ephesians 5:11 (NKJV)

Help me, Lord, to trust in you
To shun sinful habits of old
Walking each day in your righteous light
Let my witness always be bold

September 6

Glorifying Works

Let your light so shine before men,
that they may see your good deeds
and praise your father in heaven.
Matthew 5:16 (NKJV)

May all my works glorify the Lord
Let them reflect His redemption and grace
That others might turn from the darkness of sin
To the light of His forgiving face

~~~

September 7

Preach the Gospel

I have made it my aim to preach the gospel,
not where Christ was named,
lest I should build on another man's foundation.
Romans 15:20 (NKJV)

Just as Paul did in days of old
The redemption story must still be told
Lead me, Lord, as I search each day
For those who are lost and need to hear your way

September 8

Keep Jesus First

*Repent and do the first works,
or else I will come to you quickly and
remove your lamp stand from its place.*
Revelation 2:5 (NKJV)

Lord, keep my heart always open to you
That I might follow your way
Help me keep Jesus first in all things
As I work for you day by day

~~~

September 9

Go Spread My Word

"As the father has sent me, I also send you."
John 20:21(NASB)

God has said, "Go spread my word"
Don't just sit and wait
Tell the world the gospel story
That will change their eternal fate

September 10

The Greatest of These Is Love

Now abide faith, hope, love, these three;
but the greatest of these is love.
1 Corinthians 13:13 (NKJV)

God's love is always there
Sent like a heavenly dove
Sharing our burdens He strengthens us
As He shields us with His wings of love

~~~

September 11

In My Distress

In my distress, I called upon the Lord.
Psalm 18:6a (NKJKV)

I find in Him a comforting rest
In times of trouble and strife
The Lord is there to help weather the storm
A rock to anchor my life

September 12

Beware of False Prophets

*Beware of false prophets,
who come to you in sheep's clothing,
but inwardly they are ravenous wolves.*
Matthew 7:15 (NKJV)

For those who come and speak in your name
Teaching that all gods are really the same
Empower me, Lord, as a righteous believer
To recognize them, the great deceiver

~~~

September 13

Life in Eternity

He has put eternity in their hearts.
Ecclesiastes 3:11a (NKJV)

Our view is so dark and minds finite
We really cannot perceive
Our life with the Lord in eternity
We simply must believe

September 14

That I May Hear

*But your iniquities have
separated you from your God;
and your sins have hidden His face from you,
so that He will not hear.*
Isaiah 59:2 (NKJV)

Examine me, Lord, that I may see
The sins that block your word
Forgive and restore me that I may hear
The answers I should have heard

~~~

September 15

Reflecting Your Light

You are the light of the world.
Matthew 5:14a (NKJV)

Lord, may my life reflect your light
That others might find the way
To the path that leads to the cross of Jesus
Where darkness is changed to day

September 16

Blameless

*Do all things without complaining and disputing,
that you may become blameless and harmless,
children of God without fault in the midst of a
crooked and perverse generation, among whom you
shine as light in the world.*
Philippians 2:14-15 (NKJV)

Mature me, Lord, in your perfect image
Mold me so others may see
A blameless and harmless child of God
A bonded slave set free

~~~

September 17

Friends to Share

*Now Jonathan again caused David to vow,
because he loved him;
for he loved him as he loved his own soul.*
1 Samuel 20:17 (NKJV)

God has given us friends to share
The griefs and joys of life
So nurture and love the ones who care
They'll be there in times of strife

September 18

Receive Me to Glory

*You will guide me with your counsel,
and afterward receive me to glory.*
Psalm 73:24 (NKJV)

Guide me, Lord, along the way
Till life's long journey ends
That I may hear "welcome home, my son
Come rest with your family and friends"

~~~

September 19

Compassion

The Lord is gracious and full of compassion.
Psalm 111:4b (NKJV)

Show some compassion to others in need
As Jesus taught us to do
Always give others a helping hand
Someday it could be you

September 20

My Faith Is Sure

*Therefore, having been justified by faith,
we have peace with God through
our Lord Jesus Christ.*
Romans 5:1 (NKJV)

When all else fails, my faith is sure
That God is there to help me endure
Walking with me along the way
Blessed assurance of a brighter day

~~~

September 21

Joy Comes in the Morning

*For his anger is but for a moment, his favor is for
life; weeping may endure for a night,
but joy comes in the morning.*
Psalm 30:5 (NKJV)

Thank you, Lord, for another day
You have clothed me again with gladness
I praise your name for joy in the morning
You have taken away my sadness

September 22

Commissioned

For God so loved the world that he gave his only begotten son, that whosoever believed in him should not perish but have everlasting life.
John 3:16 (KJV)

We're redeemed by the blood of Jesus
Our Savior who gave His all
Commissioned believers to tell His story
We should hasten and answer the call

~~~

September 23

Bear One Another's Burdens

Bear one another's burdens, and so fulfill the law of Christ.
Galatians 6:2 (NKJV)

Lord, help me to see what others need
Instead of just seeing their sin
Then bear their burden as I recall
They're right where I have been

September 24

Be an Example

*In speech, conduct, love, faith, and purity,
show yourself an example of those who believe.*
1 Timothy 4:12 (NASB)

Help me Lord, to be an example
As I go throughout the day
For my actions speak louder to others around
Than anything I can say

September 25

Uncover Satan's Lies

*Satan himself transforms himself
into an angel of light.*
2 Corinthians 11:14 (NKJV)

Be on guard and always remember
Satan deceives and lies
But learning God's word and applying His truths
Will uncover all he tries

September 26

Follow His Lead

*If anyone serves me, let him follow me;
and where I am, there My servant will be also.*
John 12:26a (NKJV)

Lord, lead me in your footsteps
As I go along the way
Hold me close beneath your wings
As I travel through each day

~~~

September 27

Christ-like Care

*That there should be no schism in the body,
but that the members should have the
same care one for another.*
1 Corinthians 12:25 (NKJV)

Be always alert for others in need
God formed and composed it that way
The body of Christ caring for each other
In struggles and joys each day

September 28

Mold Me and Make Me

For which cause we faint not;
but though our outward man perish,
yet the inward man is renewed day by day.
2 Corinthians 4:16 (KJV)

Mold me and make me in the image you desire
Make me more like you
That I might be a useful disciple
Before my life is through

~~~

September 29

Jesus' Return

Blessed are the pure in heart,
for they shall see God.
Matthew 5:8 (KJV)

Dark trials of earth will soon be forgotten
My longings will be no more
Jesus will come and lead me to glory
To join those who've gone before

September 30

Peace with Him

*Restore to me the joy of Your salvation
and uphold me by Your generous spirit.*
Psalm 51:12 (NKJV)

We should confess and repent our sins to the Lord
And through the Holy Spirit's power
We'll find a peace as we walk with Him
Even in our darkest hour

~~~

October 1

One God

*For it was so, when Solomon was old,
that his wives turned his heart after other gods.*
1 Kings 11:4a (NKJV)

One God alone for me
One God who set me free
He paid my debt on Calvary's tree
His holy face someday I'll see

October 2

He Cares

Let your conduct be with covetousness;
be content with such things as you have.
For He Himself has said,
"I will never leave you nor forsake you."
Hebrews 13:5 (NKJV)

He's always there on the darkest days
My sadness and sorrow He shares
By His presence in the Holy Spirit
My Savior shows me He cares

~~~

October 3

Rock of Ages

Coming to Him as to a living stone, rejected indeed
by men, but chosen by God and precious.
1 Peter 2:4 (NKJV)

Though I may often stumble and fall
I'll cling to the rock of ages
Jesus will lift me and stand me tall
As I turn life's brief few pages

October 4

A Time for Everything

To everything there is a season.
Ecclesiastes 3:1a (NKJV)

A time to live, a time to die
And often between, a crying eye
A time to love and a time for strife
God remains through shifting seasons of life

~~~

October 5

Our Cornerstone

Jesus Christ Himself being the chief cornerstone.
Ephesians 2:20b (NKJV)

Jesus Christ is our sure hope
To build our firm foundation
Our cornerstone in storms of life
The One to save our nation

October 6

Your Precepts Offer Life

*I will never forget your precepts,
for by them You have given me life.*
Psalm 119:93 (NKJV)

God's words are my divine encouragement
They revive and restore my soul
In them I'll place my heavenly anchor
And trust it will always hold

~~~

October 7

Because of Calvary

*And Jesus said to her,
"Neither do I condemn you;
go and sin no more."*
John 8:11 (NKJV)

Grace alone has saved my soul
Christ died to set me free
My name is on that heavenly roll
Because of Calvary

October 8

Serve the Lord

*Choose you this day whom ye will serve;
but as for me and my house, we will serve the Lord.*
Joshua 24:15 (KJV)

We should seek to help the poor and weak
And thank the Lord but there we trod
Acknowledge and give to those who seek
For by serving others, we serve God

~~~

October 9

A Heavenly Crown

*Surely goodness and mercy shall follow me
all the days of my life;
and I will dwell in the house of the Lord forever.*
Psalm 23:6 (KJV)

He is my shepherd, the guide for my life
He restores me when I'm cast down
I run this race His promise to receive
The prize of a heavenly crown

October 10

Proven Love

God is love.
1 John 4:8b (KJV)

The love of God is so rich and pure
It was proven that day on the cross
He died for us but arose again
It was victory instead of loss

~~~

October 11

We Found the Messiah

*He first findeth his own brother, Simon,
and saith unto him, "we have found the Messiah,
which is being interpreted, the Christ."*
John 1:41 (KJV)

I met the living Savior today
And I asked Him into my heart
He gave me a new name and a job to do
Before this life I depart

October 12

What I Cannot See

*Now faith is the substance of things hoped for,
the evidence of things not seen.*
Hebrews 11:1 (KJV)

Lord, give me faith that I might follow
The path you have for me
Calm my fears and give me peace
About things I cannot see

~~~

October 13

Spread the Gospel

*But I want you to know, brethren,
that the things which happened to me
have actually turned out for the
furtherance of the gospel.*
Philippians 1:12 (NKJV)

Spreading the Gospel isn't often easy
But many have never heard
The salvation story of a loving Savior
And the freedom that's revealed in His word

October 14

All Creation

*The heavens declare the glory of God;
and the firmament shows his handiwork.*
Psalm 19:1 (NKJV)

All creation reveals the knowledge
That God is the perfect one
But knowing Him on a personal basis
Can come only through His Son

October 15

The Better Way

*Therefore I say unto you, whatever things ye desire,
when ye pray, believe that ye receive them,
and ye shall have them.*
Mark 11:24 (KJV)

Give me the faith to trust you, Lord
In all the prayers that I pray
To be assured your works with perfect timing
Are always the better way

October 16

If I Begin to Stray

How can a young man cleanse his way?
By taking heed according to Your word.
Psalm 119:9 (NKJV)

Help me, oh Lord, to recall your words
As I travel along life's way
Gently remind me and bring me back
If I begin to stray

~~~

October 17

The Strength to Persevere

But we also glory in tribulations,
knowing that tribulation produces perseverance;
and perseverance, character; and character hope.
Romans 5:3 (NKJV)

Lord, give me the strength to persevere
And keep my eyes on you
Fill me with the hope of your glory
And the faith to see me through

October 18

Relinquish

*But what things were gain to me,
these I have counted loss for Christ.*
Philippians 3:7 (NKJV)

Help me, dear Lord, to relinquish the things
That restrain my witness for thee
Give me the strength through the Holy Spirit
To become what you'd have me to be

~~~

October 19

God's Words

The words of a wise man's mouth are gracious.
Ecclesiastes 10:12a (NKJV)

Lord, give me the words when I must speak
That impart your love and grace
May the peace and truth, revealed in Jesus
Always shine full on my face

October 20

Where Is Your Treasure?

*For where your treasure is,
there will your heart be also.*
Luke 12:34 (NKJV)

May my sight be such that I might live
For Jesus and eternal things
And not for the world with its riches and fame
And the temporary comfort they bring

~~~

October 21

Tiny Mustard Seed

*The kingdom of heaven is like a grain of mustard
seed, which a man took and sowed in his field,
which is the least of all seeds; but when it is grown,
it is the greatest among herbs and becomes a tree,
so that the birds of the air come and
nest in the branches of it.*
Matthew 13:31-32 (NKJV)

Lord, give me the desire to follow your path
Wherever it may lead
Give me the faith to grow in your kingdom
Like the tiny mustard seed

October 22

Blessings and Honor and Glory and Power

Blessings and honor and glory and power be to Him who sits on the throne, and to the lamb, forever and ever.
Revelation 5:13b (NKJV)

Father, keep me singing as I wait
The great triumphant hour
When all creation will sing to you
Blessings and honor and glory and power

~~~

October 23

Ask in My Name

Whatever you ask in my name, that will I do, that the father may be glorified in the Son.
John 14:13 (NKJV)

Pray with assurance, then rest in His promise
When all your prayers are through
For Jesus has said, "Ask in my name
And anything I will do"

October 24

Back to Shore

*But when he saw the wind boisterous,
he was afraid; and beginning to sink,
he cried, saying, "Lord, save me!"*
Matthew 14:30 (NKJV)

Lord, keep my boat afloat in the storm
And quiet its mighty roar
Keep my eyes focused only on you
And bring me back safe to shore

~~~

October 25

His Forgiveness

*If we confess our sins,
he is faithful and just to forgive us our sins,
and to cleanse us from all unrighteousness.*
1 John 1:9 (KJV)

No human effort is ever enough
To cleanse us and keep us from sinning
But God has said, if we confess our sins
His forgiveness provides a new beginning

October 26

Love for Others

*Though I speak with the tongues of
men and of angels,
but have not love,
I have become sounding brass
or a clanging cymbal.*
1 Corinthians 13:1 (NKJV)

Our love for others is what people see
Our willingness to give fully free
Seeking those who hunger and thirst
Loving completely as Jesus did first

~~~

October 27

Look Within

*For the Lord does not see as man sees; for man
looks at the outward appearance,
but the Lord looks at the heart.*
1 Samuel 16:7b (NKJV)

Keep me from judging by physical appearance
That often sets others apart
But look within as Jesus does
To see what's in their heart

October 28

Priceless Treasure

*Again, the kingdom of heaven is like treasure
hidden in a field, which a man found and hid;
and for joy over it he goes and sells all that
he has and buys that field.*
Matthew 13:44 (NKJV)

The most priceless treasure one should seek
Cannot be bought or sold
But is found in the scriptures of our risen Savior
It's the greatest story ever told

October 29

His Great Mercy

*For as the heavens are high above the earth,
so great is his mercy toward those who fear Him.*
Psalm 103:11 (NKJV)

For those who love and trust the Lord
Provisions will always be there
He meets our needs in His own time
And supplies them with loving care

October 30

The Longing Soul

*He satisfies the longing soul,
and fills the hungry soul with goodness.*
Psalm 107:9 (NKJV)

Our deepest desires can never be filled
By things we find on earth
But imparted by God centuries ago
When our Savior was given in birth

~~~

October 31

A Strong Tower

*The name of the Lord is a strong tower;
the righteous run to it and are safe.*
Proverbs 18:10 (NKJV)

When troubles rush in like rolling thunder
I seek out my resting place
God, my protector, a tall, strong tower
A refuge in all that I face

November 1

Nothing Can Separate Us

For I am persuaded that neither death nor life, nor angels nor principalities nor powers, nor things present nor things to come, nor height nor depth, nor any other created thing, shall be able to separate us from the love of God which is in Jesus Christ our Lord.
Romans 8:38-39 (KJV)

Through all the temptations and earthly pleasures
That this carnal world may condone
Keep your eyes on the Lord and remember His promise
That you'll never walk alone

~~~

November 2

Like Him

When He is revealed, we shall be like Him.
1 John 3:2b (NKJV)

Lord, help me not dwell on this imperfect sinner
But the work that you've started in me
Keep my eyes on where you are
And what I'll eventually be

November 3

To Please the Lord

*Take heed that you do not do your
charitable deeds before men, to be seen by them.
Otherwise you have no reward
from your Father in heaven.*
Matthew 6:1 (NKJV)

Lord, as I strive to be a charitable servant
In all the things I do
May it not be for applause from others
But simply to be pleasing to you

~~~

November 4

Peace and Rest

*I will both lie down in peace, and sleep;
for You alone, O Lord, make me dwell in safety.*
Psalm 4:8 (NKJV)

Give me peace, oh Lord, I pray
From a world that's hostile and cold
Not just a break for my sleepless eyes
But rest for my weary soul

November 5

Great Compassion

For even the Son of Man did not come to be served, but to serve, and to give His life a ransom for many.
Mark 10:45 (NKJV)

Father, may I show compassion for others
As you have shown for me
When you died alone for all our sins
That day on Calvary

~~~

November 6

Crucified with Christ

I am crucified with Christ: nevertheless I live; yet not I, but Christ liveth in me; and the life which I now live in the flesh I live by the faith of the son of God, who loved me and gave himself for me.
Galatians 2:20 (KJV)

Bring me closer to the cross, dear Lord
Daily, where I need to be
Lift mine eyes to your bleeding brow
Where your love was poured out for me

November 7

The Greatest Gift

And to love Him with all the heart, and with all the understanding, with all the soul, and with all the strength, and to love one's neighbor as oneself, is more than all the whole burnt offerings and sacrifices.
Mark 12:33 (NKJV)

The greatest gift one can receive or give
Was given by our Lord from above
An example for us to pass on to others
He gave us unquenchable love

~~~

November 8

No Condemnation

*If our heart condemns us,
God is greater than our heart, and knows all things.*
1 John 3:20 (NKJV)

The guilt from sins of long ago
Frequently sears our mind
But receiving Christ forever frees us
From His condemnation of any kind

November 9

See God, Not Me

*Let your light so shine before men, that they may
see your good works and
glorify your father in heaven.*
Matthew 5:16 (NKJV)

I pray the things I do each day
That others around me can see
Might reflect the Holy Spirit's love
That they might see God, not me

~~~

November 10

Nothing Can Separate Us

*For I am persuaded that neither death nor life, nor
angels nor principalities nor powers, nor things
present nor things to come, nor height nor depth,
nor any other created thing, shall be able to
separate us from the love of God
which is in Christ Jesus our Lord.*
Romans 8:38-39 (NKJV)

Hold me tight, Oh Lord, my God
So I don't lose sight of thee
Keep me firmly in your grasp
All the way to eternity

November 11

The Quest for Peace

*For nation will rise against nation,
and kingdom against kingdom.*
Matthew 24:7a (NKJV)

Peace, peace, my Savior's peace
Only through Him will conflicts cease
Peace, peace, all souls at rest
Since sin came forth, it's been a worldly quest

~~~

November 12

God Is on His Throne

*Behold, I am the Lord, the God of all flesh.
Is there anything too hard for me?*
Jeremiah 32:27 (NKJV)

Be strong and confident and rest assured
That God is on His throne
He can conquer the most formidable challenge
Which means you're never alone

November 13

He Gave All

*In this is love, not that we loved God,
but that He loved us and sent His Son
to be the propitiation for our sins.*
1 John 4:10 (NKJV)

God gave His Son; His name was Jesus
He died so believers could live
The love that was shown on the cross that day
Was all that our Savior could give

~~~

November 14

The Heavens Declare

*The heavens declare the glory of God;
and the firmament shows his handiwork.*
Psalm 19:1 (NKJV)

Your majesty and glory are declared each morning
As the sun rises on your creation
Reminding us daily of your infinite love
And your grace through the cross of salvation

November 15

Living Water

But whoever drinks of the water that I shall give him will never thirst. But the water that I shall give him will become in him a fountain of water springing up into everlasting life.
John 4:14 (NKJV)

Lead me to your fountain, oh Lord
Let me drink and relieve this strife
Fill me till I'm satisfied
With your abundant water of life

~~~

November 16

Reflect

Then Moses said, "I will now turn aside and see this great sight, why the bush does not burn."
Exodus 3:3 (NKJV)

Lord, help me to stop and reflect today
On the beauty of nature you provide
Reflecting your love for all mankind
And your glory the whole world wide

November 17

He Answers Me

He (God) will be very gracious to you at the sound of your cry; when He hears it, He will answer you.
Isaiah 30:19 (NKJV)

My Savior is watching whenever I stray
By making an unwise choice
He hears my call and answers it
He knows the sound of my voice

~~~

November 18

Teach Me What to Say

Likewise the spirit also helps in our weaknesses. For we do not know what we should pray for as we ought, but the Spirit Himself makes intercession for us with groanings which cannot be uttered.
Romans 8:26 (NKJV)

Lord, when I pray and seek your guidance
At the beginning of every day
Guide me with your Holy Spirit
That He may teach me what to say

November 19

Strength and Courage

Fear not, for I am with you; be not dismayed, for I am your God. I will strengthen you, yes, I will help you, I will uphold you with My righteous right hand.
Isaiah 41:10 (NKJV)

Strengthen me, Lord, and give me courage
I feel blind but you can see
Give me rest in your arms of mercy
For my shelter is always in thee

November 20

His Witnesses

But you shall receive power when the Holy Spirit has come upon you; and you shall be witnesses to Me in Jerusalem, and in all Judea and Samaria, and to the end of the earth.
Acts 1:8 (NKJV)

We should not focus our limited time
Acquiring vast earthly treasure
We should witness to others of God's endless love
And His mercy that's beyond our measure

November 21

Led by the Spirit

*For as many as are led by the Spirit of God,
these are the sons of God.*
Romans 8:14 (NKJV)

Holy Spirit, be my guide
For this world has blinded my sight
Lead me through these darkened valleys
Back to God's heavenly light

November 22

A Willing Heart

*Give to him that asketh thee, and from him that
would borrow from thee turn not thou away.*
Matthew 5:42 (KJV)

Whenever you see an urgent need
And know you should do your part
Follow the lead of the Holy Spirit
And give with a willing heart

November 23

Clay Vessel

*And the vessel that he made of clay was marred
in the hands of the potter;
so he made it again into another vessel,
as it seemed good to the potter to make.*
Jeremiah 18:4 (NKJV)

Mold me and make me after thy will
Let me be patient, humble and still
Guide me and teach me, keep my eyes on you
That others might see Jesus in all that I do

~~~

November 24

Filled with the Spirit

*They were not able to resist the wisdom
and the Spirit by which he spoke.*
Acts 6:10 (NKJV)

Lord, fill me today with your Holy Spirit
And His power to cope with all things
Give me the wisdom to accept your grace
And the peace that submission brings

November 25

May His Glory Shine on You

*Now the Lord is the Spirit,
and where the Spirit of the Lord is, there is liberty.*
2 Corinthians 3:17 (NKJV)

Though days of darkness oft come to us
God promises to see us through
Stay close to Him and heed His words
And His glory will shine on you

November 26

The Mercy of the Lord

*Through the Lord's mercies we are not consumed,
because His compassions fail not.
They are new every morning;
great is your faithfulness.*
Lamentations 3:22-23 (NKJV)

When life around you comes crashing down
And you feel that you're utterly alone
Jesus is there as your trusted companion
Hang on, He's your cornerstone

November 27

The Raging Storm

*Then he arose and rebuked the wind,
and said to the sea, "Peace, be still!"
And the wind ceased and there was a great calm.*
Mark 4:39 (NKJV)

Daily I combat the raging storms
Brought on by sin and strife
But I'll hold fast to Christ my Savior
My hope, my anchor, my life

~~~

November 28

Be Still

Be still before the Lord and wait patiently for him.
Psalm 37:7 (NIV)

As I calmly stand still before you, Lord
With dreams that are torn apart
Give me strength and courage to wait for you
To mend my broken heart

November 29

Visions of Heaven

*And he showed me a pure river of water of life,
clear as crystal, proceeding from
the throne of God and of the Lamb.*
Revelation 22:1 (NKJV)

Visions of heaven, my goal is in sight
No earthly struggles, no battles to fight
Perfect communion with God, humanity gone without a trace
The greatest blessing received, to finally gaze upon His face

~~~

November 30

Allow Him to Lead

*Call unto me, and I will answer thee, and show thee
great and mighty things, which thou knowest not.*
Jeremiah 33:3 (KJV)

When I fail to seek the guidance of God
I falter in things I endeavor
But victory is there when I allow Him to lead
For His mercies endureth forever

December 1

Comforting Spirit

Blessed be the God and father of our Lord Jesus Christ, the father of mercies and God of all comfort, who comforts us in all our tribulation, that we may be able to comfort those who are in trouble, with the comfort which we ourselves are comforted by God.
2 Corinthians 1:3-4 (NKJV)

Thank you, Lord, for your comforting Spirit
That helps me be sensitive to others
Lest I forget during my own trials
To comfort my Christian brothers

~~~

December 2

Fruit in Old Age

*They shall still bear fruit in old age;
They shall be fresh and flourishing.*
Psalm 92:14 (NKJV)

Lord, lift me up and feed my soul
Fill me with the spirit of love
That I might continue to grow in old age
And be nurtured like a vine from above

December 3

You're All I Need

*There is none upon earth
that I desire besides you.*
Psalm 73:25b (NJKV)

Lord, guard my soul from envious thoughts
By desiring what others treasure
Knowing full well you're all that I need
And can fill my heart's full measure

~~~

December 4

Cry Out to Jesus

*And Peter was afraid and beginning to sink,
he cried, saying, Lord save me.
And immediately Jesus stretched for his hand,
and caught him, and said unto him,
O thee of little faith, why didst thou doubt?*
Matthew 14:30-31 (KJV)

We often miss the One who can help
In our despair or after we fall
Jesus is waiting, a light in the dark
He's waiting to answer our call

December 5

God Is in Control

*What strength do I have, that I should hope?
And what is my end, that I should prolong my life?*
Job 6:11 (NKJV)

When hearts are broken and we don't understand
No reasoning or person can console
Find comfort in the One who knows your grief
For God is still in control

~~~

December 6

Hope in the Lord

*Blessed is the man who trusts in the Lord,
and whose hope is in the Lord.*
Jeremiah 17:7 (NKJV)

When the storms of life threaten your godly roots
And it seems you'll be blown away
Hold fast to Jesus, He can calm the winds
He'll protect you as you bend and sway

December 7

Always the Same

*But You are the same,
and Your years will have no end.*
Psalm 102:27 (NKJV)

God is the same; He never changes
His words console my heart
He promises safe passage through the storms of life
And nothing can tear us apart

~~~

December 8

God Sees All

*If we say we have no sin, we deceive ourselves,
and the truth is not in us.*
1 John 1:8 (NKJV)

God is there; He sees it all
The sin, the grief, the lies
We may fool the world for a moment in time
But we cannot cover His eyes

December 9

A Bounty

Without Me you can do nothing.
John 15:5b (NKJV)

Barren and fruitless, nothing of value
Our work without God is in vain
But following His will produces a bounty
His spirit nourishes us like rain

December 10

Because He Lives

"He is not here; for he is risen, as he said."
Matthew 28:6a (NKJV)

Death and despair are all we receive
When we want what the world has to give
But Jesus died and covered death
And because He lives, we live

December 11

Renew Our Strength

But those who wait on the Lord shall renew their strength; they shall mount up with wings like eagles, they shall run and not be weary, they shall walk and not faint.
Isaiah 40:31 (NKJV)

When hope seems futile and your burdens are heavy
And depression creeps in like the night
When your strength is gone, turn to the Lord
And be strong in His power and might

~~~

December 12

Exalting Jesus

But what things were gain for me, Those I counted loss for Christ.
Philippians 3:7 (KJV)

The things I do throughout the day
The choices I make at work or play
Do they exalt and praise only me
Or do they honor Christ Jesus for others to see

December 13

He Sustains Me

The Lord neither faints nor is weary.
Isaiah 40:28b (NKJV)

When I am tired and weary
No place to turn or rest
I turn to God who gives me peace
He sustains me through every test

~~~

December 14

A Place Prepared

In my father's house are many mansions;
if it were not so, I would have told you.
I go to prepare a place for you.
John 14:2 (NKJV)

No human thoughts can comprehend
No dreams can ever surmise
What God has prepared for all His children
After death has closed our eyes

December 15

Ask, Seek, Knock

For everyone that asketh receiveth;
and he that seeketh findeth;
and to him that knocketh it shall be opened.
Matthew 7:8 (KJV)

We face the giants of life each day
Our frailties, our problems, our sin
Faith in God can conquer all
If we ask, He has promised to begin

~~~

December 16

Read My Heart

Hearken unto the voice of my cry, my King,
and my God; for unto thee will I pray.
Psalm 5:2 (KJV)

Thank you, Lord, for answered prayers
You know my every part
Not only do you hear my words
You also read my heart

December 17

Calm in the Storm

Jesus said to the sea, "Peace, be still!"
Mark 4:39b (NKJV)

The seas of life so often rage
We struggle to stay above
But God can calm the mightiest storm
And cover us with His love

December 18

Give Me Rest

Come to me, all you who labor
and are heavy laden,
and I will give you rest.
Matthew 11:28 (NKJV)

All my cares and all my burdens
That seem so heavy to me
Take them, Lord, and give me rest
I give them all to thee

December 19

Souls Set Free

When Jesus heard that, He said to them,
"Those who are well have no need of a physician,
but those who are sick."
Matthew 9:12 (NKJV)

Lord, help me seek out the weak and the poor
Instead of those who only help me
Make me bold to share my Savior with them
So their anguished souls can be free

~~~

December 20

Our Helper

I will pray the Father,
and He will give you another Helper,
that He may abide with you forever.
John 14:16 (NKJV)

Our finite minds seek resolutions to problems
Some griefs we cannot bear
But God has sent us the Holy Spirit
Who promises to comfort and care

December 21

God Grants Me Peace

*Peace I leave with you, my peace I give unto you;
not as the world giveth, give I unto you.
Let not your heart be troubled,
neither let it be afraid.*
John 14:27 (KJV)

Thank you, Lord, for giving me strength
Against all that the world can release
Thank you, Lord, for the Holy Spirit
Who gives me love and peace

~~~

December 22

No Worries

*For the earth shall be full
of the knowledge of the Lord.*
Isaiah 11:9b (NKJV)

No worries, no sorrow, no anguish, no fear
For Christ will have come, who loves us so dear
We'll worship His righteousness and dwell in His sight
He'll restore the world with wisdom and might

December 23

All Things Work Together

For we know that all things work together for good to them that love God, to them who are the called according to his purpose.
Romans 8:28 (KJV)

God is there no matter the storm
When all seems shambles and lost
His plan for our lives can make all things good
For at Calvary He paid the cost

~~~

December 24

You Are with Me

Yea, though I walk through the valley of the shadow of death, I will fear no evil; for You are with me; Your rod and Your staff, they comfort me.
Psalm 23:4 (NKJV)

Lord, keep me safe wherever I trod
For all this earth is your created sod
Give me peace and calm within
For I know you died to forgive my sin

December 25

A Baby Born

*For there is born to you this day
in the city of David a Savior,
who is Christ the Lord.*
Luke 2:11 (NKJV)

A babe was born, bright light was shined
Darkness retreated in fear
God's Son was sent to redeem our sins
To the cross, His journey was clear

~~~

December 26

Tell the Good News

*Sing to the Lord; bless His name; proclaim the
good news of His salvation from day to day.*
Psalm 96:2 (NKJV)

Tell the good news, tell the good news
To them who will stop and hear
Tell the good news of the salvation story
To everyone far and near

December 27

Redeem My Mistakes

And one of them struck the servant of the high priest and cut off his right ear. But Jesus answered and said, "Permit even this." And He touched his ear and healed him.
Luke 22:50-51 (NKJV)

Lord, take my mistakes and turn them around
Make them into something good
Teach me to think before I act
And to live as I know I should

~~~

December 28

He's Always There

And to know the love of Christ, which passeth knowledge, that ye might be filled with all the fullness of God.
Ephesians 3:19 (KJV)

The love of God, what can I say
His love is there through night and day
Through times of joy or endless strife
He's there for all to give new life.

December 29

Close to You

My soul follows close behind You;
Your right hand upholds me.
Psalm 63:8 (NKJV)

The trials of life seem to ebb and flow
Wherever our feet may trod
But the Holy Spirit won't allow us to break
But simply bend us toward God

~~~

December 30

The Bountiful Harvest

Always abounding in the work of the Lord,
knowing that your labor is not in vain in the Lord.
1 Corinthians 15:58b (NKJV)

Sow your seed with God's Holy word
And know that you've done your best
The Lord will produce in His own time
A beautiful, bountiful harvest

December 31

My Eyes Will See You

*I have heard of You by the hearing of the ear,
but now my eye sees You.*
Job 42:5 (NKJV)

Today we see through a looking glass darkly
But someday we'll be face to face
God will answer all our questions
When we finish this earthly race

*May those who remain after my death
Look at my life and say
He loved the Lord and ran life's race
Dependent on Him each day.*

—Billy Kyser

The Kyser Family (pictured from L-R):
Scott Kyser, Julia Kyser, Chris Kyser, Mason Taylor, Peggy Kyser, Billy Kyser, Brooks Taylor, Kim Taylor, Ken Taylor

Made in the USA
Lexington, KY
23 July 2017